"Tina has truly been giv... Church today. Her message brings God's clear diagnosis and cure for our ailing congregations. It is a word both for the body and for the individual. I have benefitted greatly from her ministry and I recommend her to you. I know her and have watched her walk through severe trials as she follows God. She is genuine, honest and transparent. There is no pretense in her. Open up your heart and let God minister to you through her. You will be blessed."

—Steve Smith
*Ministry Leader*

"This message is life changing. This is teaching that is relevant to every believer no matter where you are at in your walk with the Lord. Many people in my congregation were transformed by the anointed preaching of Tina Blount. My wife and I highly recommend this message to individuals as well as Tina herself as a powerful speaker for any church or event."

—Reverend Joseph Vosberg
*First Assembly of God, Dunnellon, FL*

"This is the best and most detailed teaching of the seven churches in Revelation that I have ever heard!"

—Dr. Gene Petty
*Former District Superintendent of the*
*Assemblies of God, Maine District*

After listening to Tina teach this message, I was motivated toward major life change. I began two different accountability/ discipleship groups in order to guard against some of the parasites from Tina's teaching. I have been telling everyone "you must read this!"

— Karen Ford, Crystal River, FL
One who heard Tina's teaching
on this subject in its' entirety.

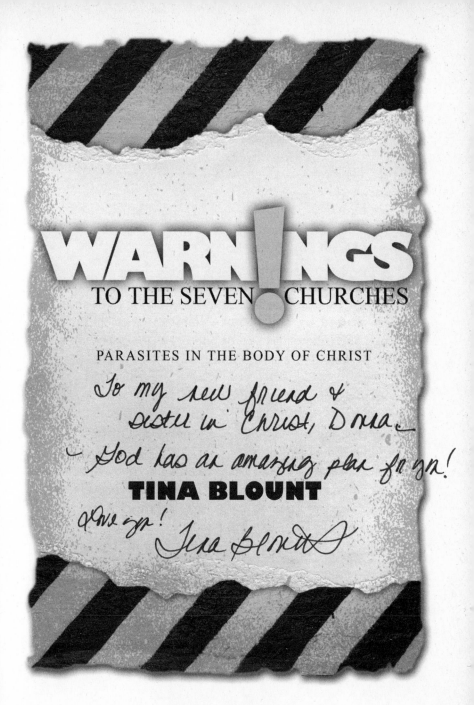

# WARN!NGS
## TO THE SEVEN CHURCHES

PARASITES IN THE BODY OF CHRIST

*To my new friend &
sister in Christ, Donna_
God has an amazing plan for you!*

## TINA BLOUNT

*love you!*
*Tina Blount*

BRIDGE
LOGOS
FOUNDATION

Alachua, FL 32615

**Bridge-Logos Foundation**
Alachua, FL 32615 USA

*Warnings to the Seven Churches:*
*Parasites in the Body of Christ*
by Tina Blount

Printed in the United States of America.

Library of Congress Catalog Card Number: 2011940875
International Standard Book Number: 978-1-61036-103-3

# Acknowledgements

There are so many people who contributed to this message being birthed. Midwives if you will who each served our Savior in their own special way. May you know that my words of appreciation will never fully convey the impact you have made on my life or the fruit your service will have on the lives of many. I am eternally grateful...

To my daughter, Jenna..
*You are truly a gift from God. Your child-like faith in the Lord and in humanity inspires me daily. I love you!*

To Katie Miller, my spiritual daughter...
*who encouraged me with the purest of faith to never give up.*

To Becky, Donna and Kim...
*Your friendship means everything to me.*

To my dear friends, Pastors Joseph and Shauna Vosberg...
*You believed in this message and me from
the very beginning. Your demonstration of love
in action sets the standard.*

To my church family at First Assembly of God
in Dunnellon...
*May you always appreciate the gift you have of being a
part of such a loving Body of Christ. Thank you for
receiving me into your family.*

To the Sunday School Class of Pleasant Grove Assembly of God, who sat under this teaching for the very first time and allowed me learn as I went...
*I say Thank you.*

To Marsha Woolley, who continues to trail-blaze the path for many of us...
*Thank you for your friendship and for allowing God to use you to open doors.*

To Pastor Ed Russo...
*for saying "yes" to a ridiculous request.*

To John Bevere and John Mason: Who said five minutes of encouragement couldn't change a life?
*Thank you for the gift of your time and encouragement.*

To the team at Bridge-Logo...
*This has been a wonderful experience. Thank you.*

To all of those who prayed, believed, edited, contributed, and encouraged...
*you have my heartfelt gratitude.*

To my Savior and Lord,...
*Thank you for choosing me, for loving me, and for dying for me. You are truly my Redeemer.*

# Introduction

As a speaker and teacher of the Word, it has become my style of communication to filter my personal life experiences through the truths of God's Word, creating real-life object lessons for others to learn from. While I am fully committed to transparency, the truth remains that there are certain things in life I would prefer to keep in the family. Do you know what I mean by the family? To me the family represents God the Father, Jesus the Son, and who could ever leave out the Holy Spirit? Then there's me—mother, daughter, sister, friend.

Some things in life should remain private, or so I used to think. However, my Father seems to have different thoughts and has taught me there are very few areas of my life that God considers to be off limits. In fact, as He so eloquently pointed out to me recently, if I have experienced something that will benefit the Body of Christ in any way, then at some point in time, no matter how personal it might be, God will strongly encourage me to share it. Well, not just encourage me; He'll burden me until I cry "Uncle" or perhaps "Abba Father."

This book was birthed out of just that kind of personal experience. An experience I would have hidden from others had the Lord not opened my eyes to its ability to communicate spiritual truths and meet us in the middle of our daily life. Like rain from Heaven, God dropped this study into my heart and it has (at least for me) taken on a life of its own. It has illuminated for me the reason that I, and many others, struggle at times to be as effective in my faith as I would desire. It has further shed light on why the Church has not been the lighthouse in a dark and dying world that it could be and should be. I pray, through the revelation of the Word of God, you will become the seed-bearing fruit tree you were created to be: healthy and strong, shining in the light of His glory.

*Tina*

# Contents

# 1

# A Worm?

"**A**re you kidding me? Are you telling me there was a worm inside me?" Those are just two of the questions I asked my doctor on one of the scariest days of my life. *Freaky* may be a better word, or even *weird*, but when all was said and done, *scary* won the contest. Yet, while scary, those words and this experience began a journey that would lead me to the pages of this book.

This wasn't my first doctor's appointment, but it was a memorable one, to be sure. In fact, my doctor and I had become, shall we say . . . friendly. One has a tendency to get friendly with someone who has operated on you three times in three years. That's right, three major surgeries in three years. Six major surgeries over ten years and now we were dealing with a worm. But I'm getting ahead of myself.

You see, over the past twelve years, I have undergone numerous abdominal surgeries in an attempt to stop scar tissue adhesions from sticking to my stomach wall. It all began with a hysterectomy gone wild because each time I was operated on to fix an internal problem, a new problem would surface, creating the need to have further operations. Each procedure became a vicious and exhausting cycle of removing adhesions, which produced . . . yes, you guessed it . . . more adhesions. So, two years ago, after exhausting all other options, my surgeon proposed a relatively new surgical procedure in one last attempt to stop the cycle.

This procedure included inserting a surgical mesh into my body that would act as a barrier between my internal organs and my stomach wall. Well, almost immediately after the surgical procedure my body developed a major infection in the wound. It was a serious infection and the doctors were concerned.

Six months later after trying every antibiotic available, it appeared as though my body was simply rejecting the mesh and the doctors reluctantly once again took me under the knife to remove it. However, they got a bit of a surprise. Under the bright lights of the operating room, they discovered a very large tissue mass about the size of an apple attached to the mesh. Upon awaking, I was told not to be concerned; it was probably just a mass of infection and a biopsy would, no doubt, reveal its true nature.

A few weeks later I returned to the office for my post-surgical consultation. When my doctor walked into the room I knew immediately that something was up. A girl can tell these things; so can a patient. As usual, he took my hand and warmly said hello and then he asked me the strangest question. He looked over his shoulder at the intern who tagged along at his heels and asked me if I would like some privacy. I remember thinking, *That's an odd question.* After all, this same intern had been in the operating room. I had been as exposed as I could get, or so I thought.

After assuring my doctor I was fine with that and his intern could stay, the doctor promptly sat down on his stool, wheeled up to me, took hold of my hands, and told me the good news was the mass was not cancer. I have to tell you this was not as comforting as it should have been, given what appeared to be a bad news option. He went to explain the bad news. The biopsy had revealed that within the mass was a degenerating parasite. That's right—a worm. A three-inch worm had been removed from my body.

"A worm?" I replied in a tone that sounded a lot like Minnie Mouse on steroids. "Yes," he responded, while squirming uncomfortably, "a parasite worm." After what seemed to be an eternity of silence, he continued to share with me that it was indeed an unusually rare parasite, only found in third world countries. After inquiring and determining that I had not been out of the country, the doctor let me know that this was no joking matter. Although truthfully, I felt like I was in an episode from the TV show *House*. You know the one where the cranky, brilliant doctor and his team work with patients with unusual diseases? Yep, that was me. Although I wasn't in a hospital, I was on my way to see a specialist, an infectious disease doctor, to be exact.

This physician reminded me of a mad scientist. He clearly was very intelligent and quite kind, but he seemed just a little too fascinated by my diagnosis for my personal taste. While he was pouring over the lab results and pathology reports, I was doing by best to be invisible. It was odd. Never before had I experienced the feelings I was now having. It was the strangest combination of fear and shame.

After reviewing my chart, this doctor confirmed I had indeed been fighting off a deadly parasite. However, it was good to learn my body's immune system had actually captured the parasite, killed the parasite, and cocooned it within the mass. He told me had it lived, it would have traveled through my bloodstream until it reached my eyes. Having arrived at that destination, it would have systematically eaten away at my optic nerve, slowly putting out the lamp in my eye, and within two years would have rendered me completely blind. Once satiated on the nerve itself, the parasite would have moved on to my brain and would have, in fact, taken my life.

That's the way parasites are. They sneak in under cover through the back doors of your body such as feet, your food, and open wounds. Once they gain entrance, they actually hide in an organ of your body, or tissue, or even in your bloodstream. They camp out just under the radar, much like a staph infection might. During moments of stress or weakness when your body begins to create blood cells to fight off the invasion, it jumps, it moves, it spreads, and that's how it makes its way through your body. Parasites are nasty little devils that gain their strength from attaching themselves to a host and, once attached, begin to drain the host of energy, nutrients, and, ultimately, life.

Since my diagnosis, I have thought about the many ways that parasite could have wormed its way into my body. My doctors theorize the parasite found in my body was more than likely attached to the surgical mesh that was inserted inside me, although no one knows for sure. They've developed this theory given the fact that the mesh itself was developed in a third world country, and parasites do not have the ability to enter the body through any means other than a back door. During a time of vulnerability that tiny microscopic worm made its way into my body and began to feed on my organs.

Six months after this experience I found myself back in the hospital, once again battling scar tissue. This time the infectious disease doctor was consulted in an attempt to ensure my parasite did not have kissing cousins. He was happy to announce that all that was left was the skin—the carcass of that nasty worm. No more traces of the deadly parasite remained in my body.

It was during this time of recovery that God began to show me how my personal experience with that nasty parasite would become a modern day parable for the Church. Let me tell you how that happened.

I had taken a bit of time off from teaching Sunday school in my home church to heal and regain my strength. A few weeks after my recovery, a friend said to me, "Tina, when are you coming back to teach again?" In that moment, I thought, *I don't know. I don't have anything in mind to teach on.* No sooner had I thought those words than I heard the Lord say in my spirit *"Parasites in the body."* I went home and said, "Lord, what exactly are you asking me to teach?" Again, I heard those words, *"Parasites in the body."*

I continued to pray, seeking God's direction, and a few days later I was in my car listening to a study on the Book of Revelation. The teacher, Nancy Lee DeMoss, referenced the letters to the seven churches in Revelation 2 and 3. Truthfully, I had never read in detail the Scriptures that describe these churches, and her words stirred my interest. A few days later, with the Book of Revelation open in front of me, God began to open my eyes. He showed me that each of the seven churches were a distinct Body of Christ. Each body, to a degree, was healthy; however, each church had unknowingly left a back door open and was in fact being infected by a deadly parasite. As I meditated on each passage, God began to call them out to me by name.

All of a sudden, it made sense. God wasn't asking me to teach about parasites in our human bodies—He was asking me to teach on parasites in the Body . . . of Christ. As I began to pour over the Word of God and study these churches, I began to see a parallel—a modern day parable, if you will.

Remarkably, every single church in the Book of Revelation represents the Body of Christ and every single member of that particular church is a member of the Body. Scripture describes each church as a golden lampstand. Each lampstand is symbolic of the Church. Each church is symbolized as the Body of Christ. Jesus himself is the power source, the light bulb that illuminates all the churches and esteems them as lighthouses in their dark communities.

Yet these churches were not shining as brightly as they were created to because they were dealing with very dangerous parasites. Parasites of such significance that the Lord himself wrote letters through the Apostle John to let them know that their back doors had been left unattended and if they did not heed His words, their lamps of effectiveness, their lamps of life would be extinguished on both sides of eternity. However, as scary as the Great Physician's report was to each church, because it was written by Jesus, a promise of healing was written with the prescription. What was the prescription? Simply stated, victory would await those who had ears to hear and hearts willing to repent.

What I have discovered in these pages of God's Word is that what was true of these first century churches is also true for us today. Underneath the current of our individual bodies and the Church body collectively, there are deadly parasites hindering the Church from being the light He's called it to be.

Recently, while watching *Life Today* with James and Betty Robison, I listened as Lisa Bevere talked about her new book, *Lioness Arising*. At one point in the conversation she told how lionesses hunt for food at night. She described how the lioness will make her way through the darkness by using the light that was created on the inside of her eyes. These eyes are, as Lisa explained it, actually "lit from within." She then related that like the lion, believers in Jesus Christ are also lit from within because the Holy Spirit makes His dwelling place inside us.

I thought about what she said for a long time that day, and later in the evening the Lord spoke to my heart. He showed me that we (like the lion) were created to be lit from within. However, the Church of Jesus Christ is not burning as brightly in the world today as it could be or should be. Because many have been infected by dangerous parasites that are actually eating us from the inside out.

That's the purpose of this book—to help you identify and root out the parasites in your own life. As you read, I encourage you to allow the Great Physician himself to diagnose and perform surgery on your heart just like He has done on mine, and use the scalpel of His Word to cut out the parasites in your life at their very core. Truthfully, the surgery can be a bit painful, but, oh, the result is worth it.

Now, I can only guess what you might be thinking. "Tina, I didn't pick up this book for me. I picked it up for the rest of the Church." Friends, if that thought remotely crossed your minds, you're in good company. Even the Apostle Peter said of the Apostle John, "What about him?" (see John 21:21). Yes, friends, this message may indeed help them, but if you are a part of the Body of Christ, why not let the Lord take a peek at your medical chart first?

If you would be a willing patient, Jesus himself will help you to become healthy and whole, shining bright in the light of His glory for the entire world to see. A world that is hungry for light, hungry for truth, hungry for Jesus.

# 2

# The Body

## OF CHRIST

Let's begin by laying a foundation and defining the Body of Christ. Before we go any further, I want you to know that laying the foundation of a message—or a house, or anything else for that matter—is the least exciting part of the process. However, most would agree that without a foundation nothing would stand. The foundation, therefore, is critical to where we are going. For that reason I would counsel you to read through this book in order and not skip ahead. We can't build or paint or decorate until we have a foundation. Ladies will understand that without foundation our makeup won't last. Men will understand that without foundation a house can't be built.

I heard a story about Michael Eisner, the CEO of Disney Corporation. As it was told to me, Mr. Eisner was building a house, a multimillion-dollar house that was expected to be a showcase for all to admire. While he was busy taking care of other details, like maybe paint or furniture, he wasn't paying close enough attention to the foundation. As a result, those in charge built the walls of the house so incredibly thin that when the roof was put on, the walls started to crumble.

The same will be true for this study. If we don't build a solid foundation of who the Body of Christ is and what a parasite can do to it, the study of the seven churches in Revelation won't be as meaningful. So again, I encourage you not to skip ahead. The study of the churches is fascinating and can be life changing, but not to the degree it could be if you don't understand how it applies to you personally.

With that in mind, who or what is the Body of Christ? To discover that answer, we'll begin in 1 Corinthians 12:12-13:

> *12The body is a unit, though it is made up of many parts; and though all its parts are many, they form one body. So it is with Christ. 13For we were all baptized by one Spirit into one body—whether Jews or Greeks, slave or free—and we were all given the one Spirit to drink.*

Now let's look at the same passage from *The Message* translation:

> *You can easily enough see how this kind of thing works by looking no further than your own body. Your body has many parts—limbs, organs, cells—but no matter how many parts you can name, you're still one body. It's exactly the same with Christ. By means of his one Spirit, we all said good-bye to our partial and piecemeal lives. We each used to independently call our own shots, but then we entered into a large and integrated life in which he has the final say in everything. (This is what we proclaimed in word and action when we were baptized.) Each of us is now a part of his resurrection body, refreshed and sustained at one fountain—his Spirit—where we all come to drink. The old labels we once used to identify ourselves—labels like Jew or Greek, slave or free—are no longer useful. We need something larger, more comprehensive.*

Based upon these Scriptures we discern three things:

1. The human body is made up of many parts; likewise the Body of Christ is made of many people.

2. Not just any people, but people who have accepted Jesus as their Savior and whose Spirit now lives (dwells) in them.

3. No matter who you are, where you came from, what you've done or haven't done, if you have accepted Jesus Christ as your personal Savior then you need to know that you are an essential and important member of the Body of Christ.

Now, let's camp here for a minute and talk about what we've just outlined. We discovered through this passage that the human body is made up of many parts, like toes, hands, a mouth, etc. The body works optimally when all of the parts are functioning in a healthy manner. To be effective, the body needs life-giving oxygen, water, and food. Our hearts need to be pumping effectively and our brains need to be engaged. Every part of the body, every organ, is contingent upon the other.

It is the same with the Body of Christ. I serve the Lord as a voice and though I may be a speaker, without the wonderful friends who serve with me as editors, proofreaders, and assistants, I would not be able to communicate the message the Lord has given me. They are essential to the finished product, and so am I. You may be a greeter in the Body of Christ, but without you who would feel welcome in your church services? You may clean the church, but without you who would want to sit in the seats? You may pastor the church, but without sheep who would need a shepherd? The Body of Christ works optimally in unity, just like the human body. It's made up of many people, but it comes together as a unit for the purpose of giving God glory.

However, it's important for you to understand that not all who sit in a church service are a part of the Body. Not all who call themselves Christians are a part of the Body. There are people all over the world who attend church regularly and have their names in church roll books who aren't actually a part of the Body of Christ.

To be a part of the Body of Christ, you must have accepted Jesus as your personal Savior and have made Him Lord of your life. It's easy to do, but at times hard to walk out. To become born again you must acknowledge that Jesus Christ is the Son of God, believe that He died a sinless death on the Cross to redeem you back to the Father, and confess that you are a sinner.

When you honestly pray that prayer and accept the free gift of salvation, the Holy Spirit moves immediately into your heart and you become a part of the Body of Christ. Without the Holy Spirit you are not a part of the living Body. You are alive physically, but dead spiritually. It is only after receiving Jesus as your personal Savior that your spirit comes alive and your name is written in the Lamb's Book of Life (see Revelation 20:11-13). This is definitely the roll book you want your name to be in.

When you make that decision, to believe in Jesus Christ and turn your life over to Him, you become a member of the Body of Christ, fully connected to God in spirit and in truth. No longer a garment on the Body, but a part of the Body. No longer a visitor in the church, but an important and essential member of the Body of Christ. You become not only an important member of your local church, but also a critical member of the Church of Jesus Christ, which makes up all believers.

I'm speaking here to the young, the old, the broken, the tossed away, the used up, and those who feel they have nothing to offer. When you accept Jesus as your Savior, He moves into your life and brings a whole basket full of good gifts—spiritual gifts that will equip you to serve Him in a meaningful way, contributing to what He wants to do right here on planet Earth. The contributions you make as a member of the Body of Christ become your eternal legacy. In thinking this through, we come to understand the fact that when we become members of the Body of Christ we become more significant, not less. On those days when we wonder, "Do I matter to anybody?" or "Does anything I do really matter?". . . remembering we are a part of something bigger than ourselves should give us hope and significance, propelling us to move forward for yet another day.

Let's keep reading in I Corinthians 12:14-26, MSG:

*14-18I want you to think about how all this makes you more significant, not less. A body isn't just a single part blown up into something huge. It's all the different-but-similar parts arranged and functioning together. If Foot said, "I'm not elegant like Hand, embellished with rings; I guess I don't belong to this body," would that make it so? If Ear said, "I'm not beautiful like Eye, limpid and expressive; I don't deserve a place on the head," would you want to remove it from the body? If the body was all eye, how could it hear? If all ear, how could it smell? As it is, we see that God has carefully placed each part of the body right where he wanted it.*

*19-24But I also want you to think about how this keeps your significance from getting blown up into self-importance. For no matter how significant you are, it is only because of what you are a part of. An enormous eye or a gigantic hand wouldn't be a body, but a monster. What we have is one body with many parts, each its proper size and in its proper place. No part is important on its own. Can you imagine Eye telling Hand, "Get lost; I don't need you"? Or, Head telling Foot, "You're fired; your job has been phased out"? As a matter of fact, in practice it works the other way—the "lower" the part, the more basic, and therefore necessary. You can live without an eye, for instance, but not without a stomach. When it's a part of your own body you are concerned with, it makes no difference whether the part is visible or clothed, higher or lower. You give it dignity and honor just as it is, without comparisons. If anything, you have more concern for the lower parts than the higher. If you had to choose, wouldn't you prefer good digestion to full-bodied hair? 25-26The way God designed our bodies is a model for understanding our lives together as a church: every part dependent on every other part, the parts we mention and the parts we don't, the parts we see and the parts we don't. If one part hurts, every other part is involved in the hurt, and in the healing. If one part flourishes, every other part enters into the exuberance.*

We find an understanding here that every single person is critical to the Body of Christ. We also find in verse 25 that if one part suffers, every part suffers. In fact, I want to focus on this word suffer for just a moment. This word *suffer* is the same in almost every translation—it's a word that means to feel pain together as a result of evils, troubles, or persecutions. As it relates to the Body of Christ, evils, troubles, or persecutions can often come as a result of parasites.

To be sure, we'll see this proved true in the Book of Revelation when one part of the Body of Christ is sick, is hurting, or is infected with parasites, the whole Body of

Christ will suffer. There's no one in the Body of Christ who is a disposable appendix. There's no one in the Body of Christ who is useless or expendable. Understanding this is foundational to our study.

Have you ever lost a member of your church family to death or tragedy? How did that loss impact your church? Did not all of you hurt at the same time? Have you ever quarreled with a brother or sister in Christ? How many were impacted by that disagreement? Have you ever had a gossip among your fellowship? How did that impact the group at large? The same theory applies here as well. When one member is infected by a parasite, very shortly the whole church is reduced in its effectiveness in your community.

# 3

# Parasites

Parasites of any kind are organisms that live on or in another living organism, known as a host. When a parasite attaches itself to a host it begins to feed. That's how it lives. It gets all its nourishment by attaching itself and feeding off another. When it feeds it grows stronger, generally as the host grows weaker. Depending upon the type of parasite, the host will experience a wide range of symptoms from a minor inconvenience to debilitating and fatal diseases.

In my situation, the particular parasite that made its way into my body would have created life-altering consequences. From having perfect vision, I would have slowly lost my ability to see light. Over time, what was clear would have become shadowy, and, eventually, I would have been rendered completely and totally blind. I was told it would have happened so gradually that, although I would have sensed something was wrong, I probably would have just excused it away until it was too late. It's still a scary thought to me. What's even more frightening is this same pattern is happening spiritually to believers all over the world and, like me, men and women, boys and girls don't even realize what's going on.

Parasites are hidden dangers that enter the body through back doors. Upon gaining entrance, either through a wound, the skin, food, or some other avenue, they attach themselves and begin the process of burrowing in for destruction. In the natural, parasites can take the form of a virus, bacteria, flea, tick, locust, or worm. Let's take a look at them in scriptural form to see an example of the harm and devastation they can cause. In Deuteronomy 28:38-42, we find this passage:

> *38 You will sow much seed in the field but you will harvest little, because locusts will devour it. 39 You will plant vineyards and cultivate them but you will not drink the wine or gather the grapes, because worms will eat them. 40 You will have olive trees throughout your country but you will not use the oil, because the olives will drop off. 41 You will have sons and daughters but you will not keep them, because they will go into captivity. 42 Swarms of locusts will take over all your trees and the crops of your land.*

This is a passage that's obviously referring to agriculture, but it's also a passage of Scripture that is describing what will happen to the Body of Christ, to believers, if they do not obey the Word of the Lord. Over and over in the Word of God, Jesus communicated spiritual truths in parables: metaphors that connect everyday life to life in the spirit. This Scripture says the farmers will be working hard but in the midst of their efforts, locusts will come and eat their crops, their vineyards and their trees, and even their children will go into captivity.

I want you to remember that it begins with just one— one worm, one locust, or one parasite. Have you ever tried to grow something in your backyard, like tomatoes or cucumbers, only to go outside and find little bugs have eaten away your vegetables almost overnight? How did that happen? The same way it says in this passage: while the farmer wasn't looking, the parasites came and attached themselves to the weakest vegetation, invited friends, grew strong, and ultimately consumed the entire crop.

Back to the parable: What was true for the farmer and field is true in the Body of Christ. A parasite of the flesh or of the enemy will often attack a weak or vulnerable member of the Body of Christ and before you know it that parasite will spread like a plague, devouring even the strong. Parasites are dangerous evils worthy of study. Let's look deeper at what parasites might look like in the Body of Christ in 2 Timothy 3:1-9:

> *¹But mark this: There will be terrible times in the last days. ²People will be lovers of themselves, lovers of money, boastful, proud, abusive, disobedient to their parents, ungrateful, unholy, ³without love, unforgiving, slanderous, without self-control, brutal, not lovers of the good, ⁴treacherous, rash, conceited, lovers of pleasure rather than lovers of God—⁵having a form of godliness but denying its power. Have nothing to do with them.*

> *⁶They are the kind who worm their way into homes and gain control over weak-willed women, who are loaded down with sins and are swayed by all kinds of evil desires, ⁷always learning but never able to acknowledge the truth. ⁸Just as Jannes and Jambres opposed Moses, so also these men oppose the truth— men of depraved minds, who, as far as the faith is concerned, are rejected. ⁹But they will not get very far because, as in the case of those men, their folly will be clear to everyone.*

WARNINGS TO THE SEVEN CHURCHES: PARASITES IN THE BODY OF CHRIST

We see these qualities out in the world, don't we? We see them on television. We see them in movies. Yet, it's important to note here the Apostle Paul isn't referring to the world, he's referring to the Church—the Body of Christ. If you look at verse 6, you will see that these parasites wormed their way into weak believers. They were men and women who weren't strong in their faith, who were loaded down with sin, and unable to fight off an attack coming through the back doors of their lives.

Now at first glance, we might be tempted to say that money or power is a parasite, but look back to verse 2 and take a closer look. Scripture says in the last days it will be people who will be the greatest parasite in the church, people who have a form of godliness but are denying its power. People will be carriers of parasites, not inanimate objects like money or buildings. One person carrying a parasite can destroy an entire congregation. You'll recognize these people by their lack of power, faith, and fruit. Not just on one Sunday, but consistently over time. You'll recognize their form.

What does it mean to have a form of godliness? Well, think for a moment what you believe a Christian looks like, acts like, and talks like. That is what it means to have a form of godliness. But it takes more than walking, talking, or acting like a believer to actually be a true believer. To call oneself a believer in Jesus Christ, you must take up your cross daily and follow Christ (see Matthew 16:24).

For a very long time I thought that Scripture meant I needed to walk around town with a gold cross around my neck. I was wrong. What it means is I must daily deny myself, crucify my own selfish desires, and obey the call of God on my life (see Mark 3:34-35). You have a call on your life too, but we'll deal with that later.

When I was nine years old, I sat beside a family friend and repeated the sinner's prayer. I acknowledged that Jesus was the Son of God, I believed that He died on the Cross for my sins, and I confessed that I was a sinner. Poof, I thought that made me a believer. There was only problem. I didn't believe it in my heart. I only believed it in my head. How do I know? Because I lived for my own pleasures every day for the next twenty years. Jesus wasn't the Lord of my life. He was the Lord of my Sunday mornings when I went to church. The rest of the week belonged to me. It took me twenty years of head knowledge and another four years of seeking until I made the firm decision I was going to let God be in control of my life. I committed to spend time with Him every single day, and as our relationship grew, I began to change. No, I didn't look any different, but I wanted different things. I desired more of God and the things of God and desired less of the things of this world. I was truly saved and was finally bearing fruit to prove it (see Galatians 5:22-23).

Friends, sadly it will be those individuals who go to church, sit in church regularly, serve in the church, yet haven't truly made Jesus Christ Lord of their lives who are used by Satan to carry parasites into the Body of Christ. Those who are in church roll books without being in *the* Book (of Life). It will be those deceived individuals who worm their way into our churches and our homes and whose lives will infect one weak believer after another until ultimately they effectively dim the light of one Christian at a time, one church at a time, one community at a time until the lampstand is completely unplugged. Am I suggesting Christians can be infected by spiritual parasites? *Yes!* A resounding yes!

So, how do we avoid this? How do we as believers develop a strong spiritual immune system so that we can capture, cocoon, and kill the parasitic spirit? After all, not one of us would willingly allow a parasite to come directly through the front door of our lives. That is the whole point of this book. To think for even one moment it can't happen to you or me is like giving the key to the enemy of our souls. It can, it does, and it may already have. You can't, even for one minute, think that a parasite can't invade your spirit. You can't get caught up in the fact that you go to church three times a week. You can't get caught up in how many Scriptures you know. You can't get deceived by how active you are in ministry. Those activities are guarding the front door. You have to protect your back door, and that is what I want you to understand through the pages of God's Word.

Remember it was in a moment of weakness, in a moment of vulnerability that the parasite made its way into my body. While I was sleeping, under the care of another, a nasty naked-to-the-natural-eye worm attached itself to an object and entered through an open door. It can do the same to you. It will be in a moment of unforgiveness or anger. It will be in the moment of unfulfilled dreams and unanswered prayers. It could be in times of passion when you are fighting for what you believe in. It could also be in times of great revival or success. Those are just some of the back doors that the enemy will come through to attack you. Every day we must recognize that we are vulnerable and take action to protect our back doors.

How do we do that? We must humble ourselves before Jesus. We must become an open book to Jesus, allowing Him to reveal to us all that He sees. We must become intentional about our relationship with Him. Not going through the motions, but passionately running hard after our Redeemer. We must become aware that our role in the Body of Christ is critical to what God wants to do on planet Earth. Because what He wants to do here has an eternal consequence. We must become conscious of the fact that God created us to do the good works He prepared in advance for us to do (see Ephesians 2:10). We must become healthy and strong with open spiritual eyes and a desire to get about our Father's business.

Beloved, parasites will kill you . . . physically and spiritually and in the process of your death, you will kill another and they will kill another and before you know it an entire congregation will be dead, leaving behind a community that doesn't know Jesus, and it will be without a lighthouse, without a lampstand.

This is serious, my friends. In the chapters to come, Jesus will reveal to us the most common parasites we in the Body of Christ will contend with. It is my deepest prayer that as you study these churches and communities with me, you will allow God himself to reflect His love to you by showing you what must be removed from your life. Would you prepare even now as I pray for you?

*Father, I thank you for every man, woman and child who is reading the pages of this book. I know that it is your heartbeat that none should perish, no, not one. I know that it is your desire that we as believers live fruitful, faithful, and effective lives. It is for this reason I have shared my story. It amazes me, Jesus, that you allowed a deadly parasite to enter into my body. You sacrificed my physical health for the spiritual health of the nations. Wow, God! Yet, that's just like you. Sacrificing Jesus for the life of all of us. So now, Father as we truly begin this journey, I pray that every individual would have ears to hear and hearts ready to respond. I stand in the gap, interceding for them even now.*

*In Jesus name, Amen.*

# 4

# Setting the Stage:

## THE SEVEN CHURCHES

There are several churches in the Bible we could study to see examples of parasites. We could look at the Church in Corinth. We could look at the churches in Galatia, Philippi, Colosse, or even the church in Thessalonica. After all, these are New Testament churches and there is much they could teach us. But truthfully, they weren't my assignment. The Lord was very specific in letting me know which churches He wanted me to study. He clearly communicated to my heart the object lesson for this message was indeed the seven churches mentioned in chapters 2 and 3 of the Book of Revelation. They are the ones that captured my attention. They are the ones that the Lord himself illuminated to me. Because it was His will, we can know for certain it will be those letters we learn and grow from, If we will allow Him, the Lord will use His letters to these churches to perform radical, supernatural surgery on us, and freedom will be the end result.

As you're reading this book, I want to encourage you to have your Bible handy and use it in conjunction with this message. It's important to me you know that although I am a woman who listens and hears from God, I will always be secondhand manna. God wants you to draw near to Him yourself. It is my hope this book becomes a tool, a bridge, and a conduit to accomplish that. But please know nothing can ever replace your own intimate time of fellowship with the Lord. With that being said, know I will always encourage you to turn to the pages of Scripture yourself and mediate on the words you find. But just in case you don't happen to be near your Bible at the time of your reading, I'll have the Scriptures here for you on these pages.

Let's begin in Revelation 1 and set the stage for our study of these churches. Revelation 1:1-3 says this:

> *¹The revelation of Jesus Christ, which God gave him to show his servants what must soon take place. He made it known by sending his angel to his servant John, ²who testifies to everything he saw—that is, the word of God and the testimony of Jesus Christ. ³Blessed is the one who reads the words of this prophecy, and blessed are those who hear it and take to heart what is written in it, because the time is near.*

Let's stop here, because it's important that we understand a couple of points before we go any further. Revelation is a book about the past, the present, and the future. It's a book about Jesus—in His past glory, in His present glory, and in His future glory. Just for point of interest, the book is called Revelation, not Revelations (as some would call it). This is important for us to know because the Apostle John, who is the author of this book, received a singular revelation of Jesus Christ. It happened in one experience, not a few experiences over several days or weeks. The word *revelation* in the Greek is *Apokalupsis*, from which we get our modern day word apocalyptic, and it means "an unveiling or uncovering."

That's an important definition because as we study the seven churches in detail, the Apostle John will be unveiling to us what was revealed to him. Jesus chose to unveil himself to John through a supernatural experience. My prayer for you will be that through the pages of this book and the Word of God, the Lord will provide you with the same kind of supernatural revelation that John experienced.

Matthew 11:27 says, *"All things have been committed to me by my Father. No one knows the Son except the Father, and no one knows the Father except the Son and those to whom the Son chooses to reveal him."* Have you ever wondered why some people seem to go so much deeper in the Word than others? Have you ever spent time with someone who seemed to have an enabling of the Holy Spirit to understand the things of God? Have you ever wondered how others seem to grow in their faith and understanding of the Bible at warp speed? This verse tells us why that happens. It's actually very simple: Because God says so. He decides to whom He wants to reveal himself and to what degree.

James 4:8 lets us know that if we come near to God, He will come near to us. We have to come near to Him first and then He'll come near us. Now, don't misunderstand me. God is everywhere. That's what's called the Lord's omnipresence, meaning He is in all places at all times. What this passage in James is describing is His manifested presence. Manifested meaning the Lord breaks through time and space and becomes tangible.

When we gain a revelation of who He is or what He is doing in our lives or the lives of others, we are experiencing His manifested presence. Truthfully, God can do that any way He wants; after all, He's God.

Who knows? Perhaps the Lord chooses to reveal himself more fully to some because they are seeking harder than others. Matthew 7:8 reminds us that he who seeks, finds. If you are going through this study half-heartedly looking for an overall knowledge of how parasites manifest in the Body of the Church, or in your husband or in your friends, then guess what? You'll get what you look for. The same applies to a serious seeker. If you want to see the parasites Jesus sees in you, then you'll have to draw a little bit closer and listen a little bit harder and let Him know you want to be rid of anything hindering you. Anything!

My friends, you can have the full and complete revelation of the Word of God if you seek Him. He will reveal himself by the measure that you seek Him. Revelations aren't usually found just dancing on the surface. Oh, you'll definitely find nuggets on the surface. The Book of Proverbs is a prime example of that, with gold nuggets in abundance. But if you want diamonds, you will have to be willing to go to some hard places in order to find what you're looking for. That was certainly true for the Apostle John since he was in a hard place when this revelation came to him—this revelation for the churches in Asia Minor then and for the Body of Christ today. Yet in spite of the hard place, He was seeking God, praising God, and fellowshiping with Him. As a result, God rewarded Him.

Now, it's in verse 3 that I get very excited about this message because it reveals to me why I believe God chose these passages for us to study.

*Blessed is the one who reads the words of this prophecy, and blessed are those who hear it and take to heart what is written in it, because the time is near.*

38

In the KJV that passage reads the time is "at hand," meaning imminent, which in turn means "is going to happen *suddenly.*" I believe that God is directing us to study these passages because the end is drawing near. All my life I've been hearing, "Get ready because Jesus is coming," but I will tell you this, I believe with every fiber of my being that His return is closer than we can imagine.

Most of us know it is going to happen—Jesus is going to come back and we need to be ready. We (individually) need to be ready. We need to get our families ready. We need to walk in such a way individually and as the Church that we lead our communities to Jesus and get them ready. We further, as the Church, need to root out the parasites we identify in our own lives through this study and in the Body of Christ so we can be healthy and strong, bearing much fruit for the Kingdom of God!

Verse 3 starts with, *"Blessed is the one who reads the words of this prophecy."* Do you know many Christians confess to not reading the Book of Revelation? It's true. I've personally heard feedback like, "It's scary," "I don't quite get it," or "We win in the end, why do I have to read it?" I get their thoughts because once upon a time I would have agreed with many of those statements.

When I was a young girl, I grew up with a pastor who often taught at prophecy conferences. Now, we didn't go to church for many years in my youth, but when my parents first got saved we went every time the doors were open. As a result my first church experiences were often traveling with my daddy to hear our pastor preach on the Book of Revelation.

My father received Christ when I was nine years old. He was a man on fire for the Lord and I remember he wanted to drink from the same cup as our pastor. If Pastor Hank went north, then so did we, and if he went to the back hills of Florida, then so did we. As a result of the prophecy teaching I had been exposed to as a young girl, I'll tell you the truth, I was afraid of the Book of Revelation. It just plum scared me. I've come to realize now that the Book of Revelation often scares those who aren't truly a part of the Body of Christ. This was true in my own life because while I had come to a head knowledge of Jesus Christ as a child, it was another twenty years before I truly gave my heart to Him. When I finally did, my love affair grew hot quickly. That passion is the fire that led me to the Book of Revelation and this time, I wasn't afraid of it. In fact, I was blessed by it.

That's exactly what this passage means when it says blessed are the ones who read this prophecy. Do you know this is the only place in the Bible that actually says you are blessed if you read what Jesus is saying? That alone should make us turn off *American Idol* and pick up the Word of God. Watching *American Idol* can make me—and you—happy, but only God's Word can make us blessed.

Not only does He want us to read it, He wants us to talk about it, to preach and teach it, and then He wants us to take to heart what we are learning. What does that mean—take it to heart? It means He wants us to take it in and nurture it. He wants us to think about it when we lie down and when we wake up. He wants us to place it in our mouths like a decadent piece of chocolate and hold it there until it fully melts and becomes a part of our spirit. He doesn't want us to just read it; God wants His word to become a part of us.

I want you to know that in the coming pages there is a very good possibility God may step on your toes through the words I have written. Yet, please know right up front that it's because of His amazing love for you. A love that is so passionate and mixed with His desire to see you and me bear much fruit. God has stepped on my toes so many times, some days I look down and expect to see nubs. A moment of discomfort and squirming that has the potential to yield an eternal glory is much greater than anything we can imagine, and well worth the pain.

Philippians 2:14-16 says,

*"14Do everything without complaining or arguing, 15so that you may become blameless and pure, children of God without fault in a crooked and depraved generation, in which you shine like stars in the universe 16as you hold out the word of life—in order that I may boast on the day of Christ that I did not run or labor for nothing."*

Remember these words, *" . . . in which you shine like stars in the universe as you hold out the word of life . . . "* because we will see them again. God want us to shine like stars for Him in our churches, yes, but also in our workplaces, in our neighborhoods, and in our communities. We can do that. It's totally possible if we are parasite-free. Yet having one or more of these parasites alive and living off of us will diminish our light and our effectiveness. They show up suddenly and without warning. Let me tell you a story of how one almost put out my own lamp.

Not long ago, one of my neighbors, who I did not know well at the time, accidentally ran her car into her brick mailbox. It was clear she wasn't injured, but the car needed a big band aid. After my husband came home from work he insisted we go see if she was all right. Truthfully, I didn't really want to go. Dinner was on the stove and I needed to be somewhere, but my husband was insistent. So, yielding to his wishes, we walked across the street to find out if she was all right.

After a brief discussion in which she assured us that she wasn't hurt and that she was simply embarrassed, I said good-bye and turned to make my way back across the street. Just as I turned the Lord prompted me to pray for her. I'm embarrassed to say that I did not want to pray for her at that moment. Very quickly I explained to God why that was. I was now going to be late for my appointment, dinner was burning, and the most obvious, I didn't even know her name. Do you think the Holy Spirit cared about my ham and scalloped potato casserole? Not one iota, so I begrudgingly obeyed and asked her quietly if I could pray for her. Her response was something I will never forget as long as I live. Without saying a word, she fell into my arms, began to sob, and said indeed I could pray, oh, please would I pray?

That moment was the start of a budding friendship. Just a simple gesture meant so much. Yet, the parasite of busyness almost kept me from shining like a star for my Jesus. Had it not been for my husband's obedience to the Holy Spirit and my submission to his leadership, that moment could have been lost forever. Do you see how easy it is to become infected? It's just that easy for me and it's just that easy for you.

One Sunday, on the way to First Assembly of God in Dunnellon to bring this message, my friend Margaret and I were driving along, talking away when all of a sudden a tree caught my eye. It was sitting among other trees in the middle of a pasture. Yet, while all the other trees were alive, vibrant, and filled with leaves, this particular tree was dead to the bone. It had no leaves, no color, and no life, yet it was standing proudly in the middle of the pasture like all of the other trees. As I began to ponder that barren tree, the Lord began to quicken my spirit and I sensed the symbolism of what I was seeing. It was as though the Lord said, "Tina, that tree is like a lot of the men and women in my house who call themselves by my name. Much like this tree they stopped producing fruit a long time ago; yet because they are so proud to be rooted in my house like this tree in the pasture, they don't even know that their spirit has died."

Are you bearing fruit for the Kingdom of God? Are you incrementally producing more and more fruit or have the parasites of life begun to eat away at your soul? It doesn't matter if you are fourteen, forty-four, or eighty-four; it's a question worth pondering. Remember, I'm not asking if you are busy. I'm asking if you are bearing fruit. I'm asking you to check your fruit to see if worms are devouring it little by little (see Galatians 5:22-23).

Going again to Revelation 1, verse 4:

*John, To the seven churches in the province of Asia:*

Here we find the Apostle John focusing his attention on the seven churches in the province of Asia. Scholars believe that this is not Asia as we know it, but probably a portion of modern day Turkey. Let me also say that scholars believe there were many churches in this area, far more than the seven listed here. Yet the chosen seven represent commonalities in the Body of Christ. Yes, each letter was written to a specific first century church, but remember the Word of God transcends time. Therefore, each of seven letters was also written for every church coming down through the ages. As was the custom of that day, they were also passed around to the other churches in the area. So, as you read the messages to these churches, please remember that what was true for the first century Church is also true of the twenty-first century Church. It was true of them and true of you and me, as well.

Let's keep reading through verse 8:

*Grace and peace to you from him who is, and who was, and who is to come, and from the seven spirits before his throne, ⁵and from Jesus Christ, who is the faithful witness, the firstborn from the dead, and the ruler of the kings of the earth. To him who loves us and has freed us from our sins by his blood, ⁶and has made us to be a kingdom and priests to serve his God and Father— to him be glory and power for ever and ever! Amen.*

*⁷Look, he is coming with the clouds, and every eye will see him, even those who pierced him; and all the peoples of the earth will mourn because of him. So shall it be! Amen. ⁸"I am the Alpha and the Omega," says the Lord God, "who is, and who was, and who is to come, the Almighty."*

I'm not going to linger here but I love how the Apostle John introduces Jesus in these letters. He refers to Him in the Trinity—God the Father, the Holy Spirit, and Jesus. He exalts Him just as we should. Then in verse 8, Jesus' words speak loud and clear and He tells us that He is the first and the last, the Alpha and the Omega, the one who is and is to come. That will be a good verse to remember in the pages that follow, when Jesus gets down to business and steps on our toes. We would be wise to remember we can trust Him because He is the faithful witness and He has the first and last words in our life. The Apostle John wants us to know we can trust Jesus. We can trust what He says to us in the letters to come. We can trust that Jesus is coming back and He loves us so much He'll do whatever it takes to ensure we will be found parasite-free when He gets here.

In Matthew 25, Jesus tells the parable about ten brides who are waiting for their groom. Five waited diligently with lanterns filled with oil, but five fell asleep and allowed their lamps to run out. Study it yourself and you'll see that when the bridegroom arrived and shut the door, it was too late for five of the brides. As they knocked on the door and said, "Let us in," the Lord replied to them, "I don't know you." Why do you think ten brides went out to meet the bridegroom and only five were allowed in when He arrived? Do you think the other five were hoping they would get in? Or is there any possibility that somewhere along the way they stopped adding oil to the flame and as a result it burned out? Perhaps, somewhere along the way, their lamps were extinguished by Warnings to the Seven Churches?

Please hear my heart; I'm not trying to scare you. What I'm trying to tell you is these women were not dumb women; they were deceived women. They thought they were going to meet the bridegroom, and yet the Lord said, "I never knew you." What happened? I'd like to suggest that somewhere along the way they stopped putting oil (faith) in their lamps. Perhaps these brides got tired, or lazy, or even busy. Perhaps they got prideful or religious. Perhaps they got parasites. What I'm saying is don't let that happen to you. Jesus says we need to take up our cross daily. We need to walk out our faith daily. It's not about working our way into Heaven; it's about believing our way there; every day, every single solitary day!

# 5

# Moving On

Let's continue reading Revelation 1:9-20:

*⁹I, John, your brother and companion in the suffering and kingdom and patient endurance that are ours in Jesus, was on the island of Patmos because of the word of God and the testimony of Jesus. ¹⁰On the Lord's Day I was in the Spirit, and I heard behind me a loud voice like a trumpet, ¹¹which said: "Write on a scroll what you see and send it to the seven churches: to Ephesus, Smyrna, Pergamum, Thyatira, Sardis, Philadelphia and Laodicea."*

*¹²I turned around to see the voice that was speaking to me. And when I turned I saw seven golden lampstands, ¹³and among the lampstands was someone "like a son of man," dressed in a robe reaching down to his feet and with a golden sash around his chest. ¹⁴His head and hair were white like wool, as white as snow, and his eyes were like blazing fire. ¹⁵His feet were like bronze glowing in a furnace and his voice was like the sound of rushing waters. ¹⁶In his right hand he held seven stars, and out of his mouth came a sharp double-edged sword. His face was like the sun shining in all its brilliance.*

*[17]When I saw him, I fell at his feet as though dead. Then he placed his right hand on me and said: "Do not be afraid. I am the First and the Last. [18]I am the Living One; I was dead, and behold I am alive for ever and ever! And I hold the keys of death and Hades.*

*[19] "Write, therefore, what you have seen, what is now and what will take place later. [20]The mystery of the seven stars that you saw in my right hand and of the seven golden lampstands is this: The seven stars are the angels of the seven churches, and the seven lampstands are the seven churches."*

There are a couple of things that I want to point out that will be relevant to our study of the churches. It's important again that we understand who Jesus is and how He is described because that description is vital to the message as He speaks to each church.

In verse 9, we are told the followers of Jesus Christ were experiencing great persecution, even to the point of being killed for their faith during this time. Christians were being slaughtered and this is why we find John exiled to the Island of Patmos. John would not be quiet about what he had seen, heard, and experienced. Therefore because the religious leaders couldn't kill him they exiled him.

We live in a world that likes to sugarcoat things. We live in a world where the gospel is often watered down and filled with sugary, non-nourishing substances. *Why is that?* I've often wondered. Could it be that the gospel is offensive in our politically correct society? Is it possible that in our zeal to step lightly on each other's toes that we've diluted the gospel, reducing it to colored sugar water? Sadly, I think so.

Yet, as I read the gospels again and again one thing continues to jump out at me. The Bible is offensive, but that didn't stop Jesus from saying, *"I am the way, the truth and the life. No one comes to the Father except through me"* (John 14:6). He didn't dance around the Pharisees, nor did He tiptoe around the Sadducees. He told the truth. That same truth is often offensive in the world in which we live. We in the twenty-first century could learn a lot from looking back to this particular time in history. We could learn a lot from observing the life of the Apostle John; after all, he was well taught by watching Jesus. I wonder if that's what kept him on his knees during his time of exile on Patmos.

A friend of mine recently was trying to get a Christian summer concert approved in her city. She shared with me how at every community council meeting their proposal had been rejected. The group that was trying to put this together prayed fervently and continued to feel it was God's will to propose this concert, so they once again petitioned the city council for permission. She told me that on the evening the council was set to meet, every other denomination in town showed up to oppose their request. She said the cults showed up and the witches showed up and the Hindus showed up and the Buddhists showed up. She said it was like a memo from hell went out and said, "If you are against Christianity, show up at this meeting."

Interestingly enough the council was open to the idea of having a concert, but were concerned that the Christian faith might be offensive to some because of the *Jesus, all or nothing* belief of the Bible. My friend was the last on the list of speakers for the petition and decided to take a radical stance. Instead of standing up and watering down the gospel, she stood up and said, "Look, the gospel is offensive, but you have to make a choice about who are you going to serve."

She made that statement knowing full well that many of the council members attended local churches in the area. She told me later it was a risky move, but it was time for her to call their bluff. After a brief recess, the council returned and delivered a verdict of *yes*. Yes, they could have their concert and they did it in such a way that it closed the door to all other religious protests.

Friends, we have to take a stand and that's exactly what the Apostle John was exiled for—taking a stand. He begins his letter in verse 9 by saying he is our brother and companion in the suffering of our faith. Are you suffering for your faith? John didn't want any praise for his exile. He wanted to be known as a fellow and common companion. Yet, we know he was not a common companion. He walked with Jesus and he talked with Jesus. So, when he said I am a companion in the suffering of Jesus, he knew what he was talking about. He watched Jesus suffer. He watched Jesus die on the Cross of Calvary. No wonder he wouldn't be quiet.

That's why I speak as well. That's why I write. I watched someone I love die who openly rejected Jesus. I was there when he took his last breaths, knowing full well he was slipping into eternal damnation. It's what drives me. It's what keeps me moving forward in spite of what others think or say.

John was suffering on the Island of Patmos. Suffering on an *island*? Most of us think of an island in terms of tropical foliage, crashing waves, and soft white sandy beaches. Maybe you even envision palm trees and coconuts. Now that you have that image in your mind, let me just say that the Island of Patmos was as absolutely contrary to that picture as you can imagine.

It is described as being a small island located in the Aegean Sea. It was about ten miles long and six miles wide and history records it as consisting of very rocky, rough terrain. It was not a day at the beach, by any means. It was not like "Exile Island" on *Survivor* where one could wander and think and pray. It was an ugly island. Commentators suggest there would be very few places where one could even comfortably rest or sit on this island because of the rocks and rough environment. That's why the Romans sent Christians there to be punished for preaching about Jesus. And yet in verse 10 John says, *"On the Lord's Day I was in the Spirit . . . "*

Now, I want us to get a picture of this in our minds. He's been exiled to a miserable island and we find him full of the Spirit. How many of us, if we found ourselves exiled for our faith from friends, family, and our church, could say, *"I was in the Spirit on the Lord's Day"*? Yet, that's exactly where he was. Some of us can't even get in the Spirit because we don't like the music or the air conditioning temperature or the person sitting beside us in God's house. Yet we see that the parasite of self-pity, complaining, and murmuring was not in him. On the Lord's Day, John was worshiping in the Spirit. The only thing he had was Jesus and it was enough. It was more than enough.

While he was in the Spirit, he heard what sounded like a loud trumpet behind him. I always think of my daddy when I hear this passage because my daddy had a voice like that. He'd call my name and it would reverberate around the house. I can only imagine what the sound of Jesus' voice was like for John. Sometimes when I heard my father call my name I knew he was just happy to see me. Other times I knew I was in big trouble. I wonder what it was like for John, exiled, alone, and worshiping? Did he scratch his head thinking the sun was too hot and perhaps he was hearing things, or did he know it was the Son of God?

Notice what happens in verse 12. John momentarily stops addressing the seven churches and begins again to talk to us. It's almost like he's saying, "I cannot tell you any more of what God told me to say until I tell you what He was like! What it was like to behold Him with my own eyes in all of His glory." John says, *"I turned around to see the voice that was speaking to me."* He turned to see the voice and who it came from; the voice that probably made every hair on his body stand at attention; a voice that thundered so powerfully through the air he had to turn around to find its source.

Have you ever had a moment like that; when God broke into your mind and heart with His words? While I have communed with God on many occasions I did have one experience that perhaps came close to what John experienced. Only once so far in my life. I had gone to the movies with two of my girlfriends and my daughter Jenna. The movie was one you might have seen before called *The Pursuit of Happyness*. While watching the movie a holy cry came over me I could not explain. While certain scenes of the movie were sad, my emotional reaction was much deeper than what those scenes called for. At one point about midway through I even had to leave the movie theatre and go to the restroom in order to pull myself together. I remember standing in the stall and saying out loud, "God, what is wrong with me?"

After regaining my composure, I returned to my seat only to lose it all over again and found myself coming unglued, inappropriately so for what was going on in the movie. It was during this last emotional breakdown I heard an audible voice say these words, "Help my people, help my people." It was so clear and so loud it sounded as if it were literally coming out of the sound system. The words so shocked and seized me that I grabbed hold of my girlfriend to the left, asking if she had heard it too, and she replied by shushing me. I squeezed my girlfriend to the right and asked if she had heard it and, yes, she shushed me too.

I needed to know if someone else had heard it so in frustration I looked up behind me and there sat three nuns.

Surely if it was God they would have heard it, too, but before I could even ask the question they firmly asked me to be quiet. I will tell you in that moment, even without confirmation from my friends or the nuns, I knew that I had heard the audible voice of God. That voice had such power and authority and touched someplace so deep inside of me that I have never been the same. It ruined me for anything or anyone else. That voice—pure, beautiful, thunderous—was just for me. That voice, that pure, beautiful, thunderous voice, was for John; but not just for John—for you and me, too.

John says in verse 12 that when he turned to see the voice he saw seven golden lampstands, which represent the seven literal churches in the seven different cities we are going to study. He continues writing that he saw someone *"like the Son of Man"* standing among them. Now, let me just say John knew who Jesus was. He had walked with Him, talked with Him, and spent time with Him while He was in his natural human body. But remember, John had also experienced Jesus in all His glory when He was transfigured on the mountain in Matthew 17. So, I wonder if that's what John means when He says, *"like the Son of Man"*? I wonder if he's saying, "What I saw looked just like my memory of when Jesus revealed himself to Peter, James, and me in all of His glory." He was overwhelmed. In fact, going ahead to verse 17, you'll see when He saw Jesus standing among the lampstands, he fell at down as though he was dead (much like the disciples' reaction in Matthew 17).

John says in verse 12, *"I turned around to see the voice that was speaking to me."* I love how commentator John Darby describes this passage in his *Synopsis of the New Testament*:

> The same voice that afterwards called John up to heaven, He now hears behind him on earth—the voice of the Son of man. It summons his attention with

power; and turning to see the voice, as Moses towards the bush, He sees, not the image of God's presence in Israel, but the vessels of God's light in the earth, and a complete summary of it all, and, in the midst of them, Christ as Son of man.

When was the last time God spoke to you like that and got your attention? I don't hear God out of sound systems every day, but even in the quietness of my spirit His voice has the power to captivate me. He wants to do the same for you.

I love the way it says Jesus stood among the golden lampstands. In verse 20 we are told these lampstands are the seven churches John is going to write to. I love the fact that not only did John see them as golden, but also Jesus himself calls them golden. It is really important that we break down what it means because it will frame the reference for what God desires each of these churches to become, and more importantly what it means for us to become.

The lampstands were golden because God himself is pure gold. It was His image reflecting and illuminating them. We know that because verse 13 says that standing in the middle of them was someone *"like the Son of Man."* Take a moment to see the picture in your mind: seven lampstands glowing from the overwhelming radiance reflected off of Jesus' face. No wonder they were called golden. Friends, God wants us to be walking, talking, breathing lampstands reflecting His character and His love and His holiness to a lost and dying world. He longs for the Church collectively and you and me individually to shine brightly as lampstands in our communities.

Matthew 5:14 says, *"You are the light of the world. A city on a hill cannot be hidden."* God's Word says you are called to be light in your family, your office, your school, your church, and everywhere you go in your community. You may not feel like a light. You may not be acting like a light, but if you have accepted Jesus' gift of salvation that's exactly what you are: a light. In this passage, as well as our key text in Revelation, Jesus says He's standing in the center of His Church giving it power and light. He is the life-giving power of the Church, of the Body of Christ. You, my friend, are that Body. You are the Church. The building we worship in is called a church, yes, but the Word of God calls you His temple because that's where His glory lives. If we hide that light under a bowl, as the illustration continues in Matthew 5:15, then who will be light to the world? Jesus has decided to reveal himself through you and me. There is no other plan; we're it!

I know there are days when you don't feel like being a golden lampstand because there are days I don't feel like being one. I had a day like that a few months back. I had been on the road traveling for a month-long speaking tour and returned home fulfilled, but physically and emotionally spent. We had been driving from Miami to Jacksonville and my body was letting me know it needed some tender loving care. I decided a bit of pampering was in order so I scheduled a massage with the intention of lying on the table and not saying a word. On this day, I wanted to put a bowl over my lamp (or a sheet, in this case) and simply rest. My massage therapist, on the other hand, had other intentions and very quickly I was to learn, so did God.

Almost as soon as the lights dimmed, the talented woman who was giving me the massage attempted to engage me in conversation. I have to be honest; I was frustrated. As she continued to ask questions hoping for a meaningful conversation, I began to complain to God in my spirit that I was tired. I had been working hard for Him, and I really just wanted to rest. For a moment—a brief, delicious moment—she grew quiet and then, just when I thought God had answered my prayers, she blurted out, "My husband is supposed to find out if he's going to lose his job today."

I will tell you the God's honest truth; in that moment, I got mad. I thought, *Oh no, Lord, You did not.* You see, very few conversations are as near and dear to my heart as helping someone find new employment who has been unemployed. In fact, I had just released a book entitled, *Now What? Finding life through a layoff and a job, too,* a month earlier. Not only had I released it, that's what I had been speaking on for the past month. In that moment, I knew God had just reached down into my pamper time and had firmly let me know that I do not ever have the option to hide my light under a bowl or throw a sheet over my golden lampstand.

This woman needed to be ministered to. She was scared, she was worried, and she needed Jesus. I, on the other hand, was tired, frustrated, and, by the way, did I mention I was also naked? Lying on that massage table covered by only a sheet. Yet, God didn't care. He wanted me to tell her about His love for her and His desire to help her in this season of her life. Out of obedience to the Lord, I began to truly listen to her heart and as we talked I learned her husband was an atheist and she had serious questions about God herself. Over the next twenty minutes I had the wonderful privilege to lead her to Jesus.

At one point she was weeping so hard her head was on the table between my ankles. I can remember sitting up, wrapping my little sheet around me, and leading her in the sinner's prayer. When she prayed, the glory of the Lord filled that room. It was an experience I will never forget for as long as I live. And yet, I almost allowed a parasite of selfishness to dim my lampstand to the point where it held no power and revealed no light.

Looking back to our Scripture, the Apostle John lets us know through the description of his revelation of Jesus that He alone is the light-giving power source for us individually and the Church collectively. He lets us know through his words that the sight he saw was beautiful. The sound he heard was powerful. The revelation he received was transformational.

When God spoke to my heart that day in the movie theatre He ruined me for anything and anyone else. I heard the voice of my Lord. I heard His command. He commanded me to help his people. He's commanded you as well. Go and share the good news of the gospel.

That's our order, that's our mandate, that's why we're to run our race. That's why I wrote this book: to help us all learn from the churches of Asia Minor the kinds of parasites that can get into our lives, dim our lights, reduce our effectiveness, and destroy our fruit.

You see, the word *parasite* comes from a Greek word that literally means "One who eats off the table of another." In the human body, a parasite will eat off the food, organs, and tissues of a person, leaving them weak and, given enough damage, near death. As the Body of Christ, you and I are charged with producing much fruit, with being salt and light, but we can't do that if we are being eaten alive by spiritual parasites.

After seeing Jesus in this way, standing in the middle of the lampstands, I wonder if the Apostle John could relate to Matthew 5:14, which says that believers are to be the light of the world. You are the light of the world. Yes, you! I've said it before and I'll say it again with emphasis: you may not want to be a light or think you're acting like a light, but that doesn't change the way God sees you. I've heard it said God doesn't have a Plan B. It began with twelve disciples and grew from there. You are the light on a hill in your community, in your workplace, in your nail salon, yes, even in your fishing hole.

But only if you're willing to say *yes* to whatever the Lord asks of you.

Are you willing?

# 6

# What Does

## GOD LOOK LIKE?

"What do you think God looks like?" I'll never forget when my daughter Jenna asked me that question. It was the day after her father had died and we had gone for a long walk. The sky was gray and it matched my mood, but Picaboo, the family dog, had energy and Jenna had questions. Jenna was four years old and I remember thinking it an odd question. I was ready for "Where did Daddy go?" I was ready for "Why did daddy have to die?" But "What does God look like?" That question caught me by surprise.

I don't really remember exactly how I answered her at the time but I do remember wondering why she wanted to know. Much later I realized that to Jenna what God looked like was relevant to her understanding of what was happening. She needed to picture God in her mind to help her understand the situation. She understood enough about God to know, even as a four year old, that God is in control of everything. As a result, she wanted to "see" the one in control in her heart and in her mind.

Now let's apply that to the Scripture we are looking at in Revelation. What God looks like to the Apostle John is as relevant to us as what He says. It's from these next few verses Jesus will describe himself to each church through the ink of His letters. Here in verses 13-16 we find our answer.

We see Jesus " . . . *like the son of man, dressed in a robe reaching down to his feet with a golden sash around his chest.*" This passage lets us know Jesus is royalty. He is clothed in the garments of the Old Testament High Priest because in Heaven He performs the ministry of intercession for you and me. When Jesus is interceding for you and me, this is what He looks like. While you are reading this book, He is interceding for you. When you begin to awaken to the parasites that have been hindering you, it will be Jesus who will be interceding for you (see Hebrews 7:25; Hebrews 4:14).

Over the past few months I have been walking through a very difficult season personally. It has been indirectly a result of the writing of this book, yet it has fingers and toes that touch many other areas of my life. Friends have been good to send me little words of encouragement in the form of cards, each one ministering to my wounded heart and mind. The other day, on a particularly difficult day, I went to the mailbox and saw the familiar handwriting of one my friends. Not wanting to wait another moment, I stood outside my home and quickly ripped the envelope open. Indeed, there was a card inside and it simply said, "I am praying for you and so is Jesus."

While the breeze ruffled my hair, I intentionally closed my eyes and pictured my Savior dressed in his royal robes, sitting at the right hand of the Father making intercession for me (see Acts 2:33). I pictured Him asking our heavenly Father, to comfort my broken heart, to heal my confused mind, and to meet every tangible need of the day (see Romans 8:26-27).

Dressed in a royal robe with a golden sash around His chest, that's my Jesus, that's your Jesus, ready and willing to intercede for you. If you haven't pictured Him that way in a long time, or maybe ever, I invite you to take a moment, close your eyes, and see your Savior in your mind's eye as the King He truly is, interceding for you.

*"His head and hair were white like wool, as white as snow, and his eyes were like blazing fire."* John's description coincides with the vision of Daniel (see Daniel 7:9) in picturing Jesus' holiness. His blazing eyes indicate the righteous anger He feels because of the sin He is speaking of to these churches, and how sin cannot enter into His holy presence. We see here a picture of His holiness and purity. If you would like to read further into the passage in the Book of Daniel, you will see God seated on the throne with the books opened around Him judging the world.

Remember that in the pages to come as the Lord speaks to each church. God is a loving God but because He is pure and holy by His very nature, He cannot tolerate sin. When He looks into your heart and shows you a parasite or two, I encourage you not to get angry with Him. Just know that through the eyes of blazing fire He is righteously angry that anything impure is in your life because it hinders you from being who He created you to be (see 1 Thessalonians 2:13). When He reveals behaviors that are the result of the worms which are trying to sneak through the back door of your life, remember the Lord desires you to be holy just as He is. Feel safe, beloved, because He will never accuse or condemn you as the enemy does, but with the love of Christ He'll guide you as only a perfect Savior can.

*"His feet were like bronze glowing in a furnace and his voice like the sound of rushing waters."* The sweet feet of Jesus, the feet that carried the Cross up the hill of Calvary. The feet that bring good news of hope found in His death, burial, and Resurrection. Those same beautiful feet also

represent judgment—judgment for all of mankind who have not placed their wholehearted faith in Him. Coupled with His voice reminiscent of rushing waters, indicating that the Lord's judgment will happen suddenly (see Revelation 19 and 20). When He returns quickly to the Earth, make no mistake: there will be judgment on Earth. For over 2000 years, God has given every single person time and opportunity to accept Jesus as Savior. He has given us time to not only come to a saving knowledge of His love for us, but also instruction for living in holiness and victory.

This book was not written for the unsaved, the lost, and those who have never heard of Jesus. I believe this message is for those in the Church who call themselves believers, yet live according to their own standards and are ruled blindly by their own carnality. The Lord gave me this message as a reminder that judgment will come like a thief in the night. Friends, I don't want to be here when it happens and I don't want you to be here, either. The Lord's voice, like rushing waters, reminds us that His Word is a living, breathing, and active sword moving quickly over the Earth and reaching into the most intimate places of our lives. Should you hear the voice of the Lord in your spirit as you read this message, please don't explain it away, but close your eyes and allow Him to lead you into a prayer of repentance, cleansing you with those same living waters.

*"In his right hand he held seven stars, and out of his mouth came a sharp double edged sword."* We see that the stars are the messengers of the seven churches and represent the pastors of each church written about in Revelation 2 and 3. Through this passage, God is showing us that He holds them in His very hands. He esteems them and uses them as He sees fit. They are connected to God the Father and are indeed His very hands.

Just yesterday I received an email devotional written by someone who reduced a man or woman of God called into full time shepherding to nothing more important than a builder or gardener. While I mean no offense to the builder or gardener, I must sharply disagree with the opinion of the writer. A man or woman of God called by the Lord to lead others safely to the promised land of Heaven has the most important role on Earth, in my humble opinion. They are called by God to be watchmen on the walls, fighting off the enemy, and nurturing the flock to do the perfect will of God. In verse 16, by holding up the pastors and revealing in the same sentence that a sharp double-edged sword is coming out of His mouth, the Lord is letting us know that He holds up the pastors to speak His Word with power.

This sword described in Hebrews 4:12 is the one that lets us know that the Word of God is living and active and cuts through all the bologna in our lives. It removes the mask that many of us try to put on. It's double-edged because it brings both comfort and conviction. One without the other will leave us unbalanced. This balanced approach to the Word is what Jesus is empowering the pastors to bring forth. To speak a word that addresses sin, but also reminds us that through repentance redemption is available to everyone. We need both words at the same time and right here we see that a pastor, anointed and responding obediently to the call of God on his life, will communicate both.

*"His face was like the sun shining in all its brilliance."* Lastly, we see Jesus' countenance, His demeanor, His face shining like the sun, fully transfigured, much like the Transfiguration in Matthew 17:2, and at the Great White Throne Judgment in Revelation 20:11-15. Transfigured; it means to be changed into a divine nature. The Apostle John didn't see just another human being before Him. He saw Jesus in all of His glory.

I love what it says in verse 17. When John saw Jesus in His transfigured glory, he fell at his feet as though dead. Totally out, knocked down, and overwhelmed by the beautiful power of God. I wonder what might happen if, before we utter another word to the Lord, we could imagine ourselves standing before Jesus as John did. How might that visualization of Him in all His glory change our communication, our worship, and our praise? Would we still offer half-hearted prayers during times of busyness, or would it change our relationship with Him forever? I wonder . . .

Yet in spite of the awesome experience John had just witnessed, verses 1-20 tell us how Jesus goes on to encourage John to not be afraid, but to do what he has been asked to do. Friends, John had an assignment to write a letter to each of the churches in Asia Minor. To encourage, rebuke, and root out parasites. I have a similar assignment and am fulfilling it by writing this book. Are you ready for surgery?

We've taken time to understand what Jesus looked like because He wants to be known. It's so much easier to receive a word of rebuke or even a word of encouragement from someone you know. That is why, I believe, Jesus takes time here to show himself to John in this way. In my home church, I've been teaching a series entitled "If, Then" based upon 2 Chronicles 7:14 which says, *"If my people who are called by my name would humble themselves and pray and seek my face, then will I hear from heaven, I will forgive their sins and heal their land."* Right there, God is letting us know He wants us to seek His face, not just His hand. He wants to be known, and through Jesus we can come to know Him. We serve a living God. Because He's alive we can have an intimate relationship with Him. As a by-product of that intimate relationship we can know that when God speaks to us we can trust what He says.

So, in the pages to come, if God begins to speak to you about a parasite that is robbing you of becoming the man or woman of God you were created to become, don't close the pages in fear or doubt or anger. Draw closer to Him and allow Him to speak to the deep recesses of your heart and life. His Word promises us in James 4:8 that if we will draw near to Him, He will draw near to us.

I'll never forget visiting a church where I was going to speak and one of the elders let me know he didn't much like women preachers and didn't think I should be bringing the message. Although his comment hurt me, it didn't change me because I didn't know him and he didn't know me. Now, should God ever say that to me, I'd be listening much more intently because He does know me. This man was speaking out of His bias, but God does not have a bias. His only desire is for me to spend eternity with Him and bring as many friends with me as possible. You can trust Him when He speaks to you.

As we begin to study the seven churches in Asia Minor, will you seek God's face? Will you tell Him you want to know Him, and ask Him what He sees in your life? This time of preparation is critical to what is to come. I invite you to close your eyes and picture the Lord of lords and King of kings as He's pictured here in Revelation. When you do, begin to pray to Him, asking Him to prepare your heart for the work He wants to do in you. Then be still and let Him talk to you and whisper to your heart how much He loves you.

# 7

# Ephesus

As we get ready to read our first letter to the Church of Ephesus, I want you to keep several important factors in mind.

First, these are seven actual letters that were written to seven actual churches located in different cities throughout Asia Minor. Second, these letters were addressed to the seven pastors within the seven churches with the expectation that he would read them to his congregation and address the issues at hand. Third, they were messages that were circulated throughout the region for the benefit of other churches as well. Fourth, remember that God's presence dwells within us and we are the Church. That means that these letters were not just applicable to those in the first century churches, but to us individually and collectively today as the twenty-first century Church. Lastly, there was general way that Jesus communicated to each of the churches. He used what I call the Oreo cookie communication method.

If you can imagine an Oreo cookie in three layers, you'll come to see in Jesus' letters that He often provides feedback in the following format: affirmation (top cookie), rebuke (double stuff), call to repentance mixed with guidance and direction (bottom cookie). In fact if we look to God's Word for direction, we'll almost always find this Oreo cookie approach. Let's get started.

## To the Church in Ephesus

We will begin by reading about our first church, the Church of Ephesus in Revelation 2:1-7:

>¹*To the angel of the church in Ephesus write:*
>
>*These are the words of him who holds the seven stars in his right hand and walks among the seven golden lampstands:* ²*I know your deeds, your hard work and your perseverance. I know that you cannot tolerate wicked men, that you have tested those who claim to be apostles but are not, and have found them false.* ³*You have persevered and have endured hardships for my name, and have not grown weary.*
>
>⁴*Yet I hold this against you: You have forsaken your first love.* ⁵*Remember the height from which you have fallen! Repent and do the things you did at first. If you do not repent, I will come to you and remove your lampstand from its place.* ⁶*But you have this in your favor: You hate the practices of the Nicolaitans, which I also hate.*
>
>⁷*He who has an ear, let him hear what the Spirit says to the churches. To him who overcomes, I will give the right to eat from the tree of life, which is in the paradise of God.*

Ephesus was the first of seven churches that Jesus addressed as being one of the seven golden lampstands. Now, I want you to remember these weren't the only churches in this region; in fact, we are told through the commentaries there were somewhere between 500 and 1000 churches in this area. But Jesus chose these seven to write to and referred to them as lampstands called to reflect His light to the communities in which they were located.

Let me suggest that it's reasonable to assume Jesus selected these seven churches to illuminate the most common parasites in the Body of Christ. While it is natural and normal to study a passage of Scripture like this from afar, I continue to invite you to allow God's presence to make this study personal to you. For it's in that place of intimacy with Him where He alone can show you, not only what existed in the Church of Ephesus, but also in the church within your heart.

Ephesus was the most prominent metropolitan city in the Roman province of Asia. History records that Ephesus was a city of between 250,000 and 500,000 people, so we can safely conclude that this was no small town. It's important to understand each church is called to be a lighthouse, or a lampstand, within its community. So, in order to fully comprehend what is going on within the church, you need to understand what it was like to live in that city. You'll see that parallel in every church we discuss. I hope you'll also see the parable for your life and community as well.

Ephesus was a city with culture. It had Roman culture because of the government, but it also was strongly influenced by the Greeks. The Greek influence brought in a strong appreciation for drama. If you were a visitor in Ephesus it would be common for you to walk down the street and see a Greek play being acted out on the steps of a nearby building. In addition, people in Ephesus were rarely bored because Olympic-like sporting events were held year-round to entertain its citizens. This was a city that had money and as such created an environment where activity and fun were always available for purchase. The Roman government knew these entertainments were revenue streams and so encouraged the Ephesians to actively participate. Given that Ephesus was a seaport and ships came in daily with cargo and lonely crews, the more activities the city offered, the more business and revenue they could acquire.

This was the place to live if you wanted to be in the hub of activity. This was no suburb or small town, but a big metropolitan city. I live in Brandon, Florida. It's a nice area that caters to families. Yet, it's not what I call a "happening" city. For that I would need to drive into Tampa. Tampa is a city that offers culture, NFL football, major league baseball, fine dining, and Broadway plays. It's an active city near a port, similar to the city of Ephesus.

Now this particular city had a very strong Christian presence; in fact the Church of Ephesus was birthed out of Pentecost. Scholars believed it was the Apostle Paul himself who originally brought the gospel there. In fact, in Acts Chapter 19 you'll find that Paul ministered there for two years.

But in spite of its strong Christian presence, the city had a problem. It was known to be an epicenter for occult practices and idol worshiping. It wasn't underground, either. Not like today where Christianity might be the "community faith," while all other beliefs are practiced after dark. No, in Ephesus the occult practices competed for the attention of Christians and unbelievers alike.

Within the city limits of Ephesus stood a temple that had been built to the Greek goddess Diana, who was known as the goddess of fertility. As a result people came from all over the region to pray and seek her face in an effort to resolve and be healed from fertility issues. Not only did people come and pray inside the temple, but also ate food sacrificed to Diana there. If that had been the only sin it would be bad, but it was also expected of someone visiting the goddess of fertility to participate in sexual activities and other occult practices in honor of her name. It was common practice and no shame was associated with it, as these sinful actions were thought to bring about healing.

This was not a city where you would want to plant a church, but it was certainly a community for which missionaries would have a burden. This was not a city where you would want to be a Christian business owner because to choose not to worship Diana would have been very bad for business.

In spite of all of the idolatry and witchcraft, the Christian church was indeed growing. You see, Paul brought the message of the gospel with such passion and zeal that many people were being saved and the Church of Ephesus was budding. In fact, you'll find that the Apostle John, who is penning this letter on behalf of Jesus, even pastored this church for about three years, while writing I, II, III John. The church grew because passionate men and women of God ensured the gospel would go forth in spite of what was going on in their community.

Yet it was because of the very heart of the Christian message that a rift was created between the church and community. Prominent business owners were not happy that Paul, John, and others were preaching the gospel, because the message of "no idols" and serving the one true God alone was bad for business.

It was especially bad business for the silversmiths, who had a very specific job to do. They were to make the idols to be worshiped in homes and businesses. When Christianity came into the area and Paul and John began to renounce idolatry, they began to teach the new believers how to root out the idols both in their lives and on their shelves of their homes. They were taught to melt them down on the streets of Ephesus and to serve only Jehovah God himself.

As you can imagine, the rub came in the form of money. To put it bluntly, Christianity was impacting the business owners' checkbooks, and that was a problem. Together the temple priests and the business owners decided that Christianity and Paul had to go and decided to run him out of town. They did, but not before he brought together a group of elders and instructed them how to continue living out their faith in spite of the community in which they were located.

If you would look with me at Acts 20:25-31, we'll be able to see at a glance into the instructions the Apostle Paul gave to the elders in Ephesus:

> *25Now I know that none of you among whom I have gone about preaching the kingdom will ever see me again. 26Therefore, I declare to you today that I am innocent of the blood of all men. 27For I have not hesitated to proclaim to you the whole will of God. 28Keep watch over yourselves and all the flock of which the Holy Spirit has made you overseers. Be shepherds of the church of God, which he bought with his own blood.*
>
> *29I know that after I leave, savage wolves will come in among you and will not spare the flock. 30Even from your own number men will arise and distort the truth in order to draw away disciples after them. 31So be on your guard! Remember that for three years I never stopped warning each of you night and day with tears.*

He tells them he had done the work of the Lord and it was time for him to take the gospel to another community. He was commissioning them to take care of each other and the Church of Ephesus. He further warned them to keep watch for the wolves outside the church walls and from within their congregation, as well. He's cautioning them, *". . . be on your guard!"* He warned them to protect, not only their front doors, but also their back doors.

Paul was warning them about parasites. Remember that parasites are those organisms that attach themselves to the host and feed off of the body until it has no strength left. Here we see how Paul prophetically told them where the parasites were going to come from. They were going to rise up outside the church—in the form of business owners and occult leaders—and they were also going to rise up inside the church, as wolves in sheep's clothing. Again, Paul, under the anointing of the Holy Spirit said, *". . . be on your guard!"*

Now let's break this down a little further because it is incredibly easy for a parasitic enemy to slip in through the back doors of our lives and churches if we are not on *our* guard! Notice that Paul first urges them to be on guard regarding their own lives and then the lives of their flock. He was talking to the pastors and he wanted them to know that before we can help others root out the parasites in their lives we must allow the Holy Spirit to look into ours. It would be so natural to read this book and begin to think about the others in your life who also need to read it. It would be easy to identify a potential parasite in a friend or family member's life. While I would like for you to pass this book on to as many people who will read it, it's more important that you take personal action first. We all have a sphere of influence. But we shouldn't look outside until we look within. That's what Paul was saying to them. He was pleading emphatically, with tears, for them not to be so super-spiritual that they themselves became vulnerable to Satan's snares.

This warning found in the Book of Acts for the elders of Ephesus occurred some thirty years before Jesus' letter to this church. Interestingly enough, I don't believe Paul knew what was going to happen, but he knew enough in the Spirit to see a pattern emerging; a pattern that burdened him to tears. We know that Paul wrote this passage under the anointing of the Holy Spirit. God used him to warn the Church of Ephesus about the parasites that would rise up in the form of people, from not only outside the church, but also from within. Most would understand an enemy could come from outside the building of the church, but inside? Yes! Because the building is filled with the people who live in that community.

This would be a great time to remember: we go to a church building, but the only reason it's called "the church" is because the Church—you and me—show up. Otherwise it would just be a building. God's presence can dwell anywhere, in anything, but it lives in His people. The people who come to church may be the Church or they may just be sitting inside the church building.

Now, let's turn back to our text in Revelation to see if the elders heeded the instruction of the Apostle Paul some thirty years before they would have received the letter from Jesus.

## The Oreo Cookie

Remember that God has this amazing way of giving us feedback in the form of an Oreo cookie. In this passage, Jesus is about to give this church a layer of *affirmation*—affirming them for what they have done right. Then He will give them a single or double stuff helping of *rebuke,* communicating to them about an area that needs to be addressed. Then after calling them to repentance, He will conclude by providing the solidity of *encouragement and direction* that will get them redirected onto the narrow path again. I encourage you to pour a glass of milk and let's see what our Oreo looks like.

## The Affirmation

Let's study the affirmation to find out what this church body was doing right. The Lord begins by reminding them who is writing the letter. I love how Jesus just sets the stage:

> *"To the angel of the church in Ephesus write:*
>
> *These are the words of him who holds the seven stars in his right hand and walks among the seven golden lamp stands:"*

In everyday language he was saying: "Dear Pastor, This is Jesus. Now listen up." He's talking to the pastor because we remember when Jesus is holding up the seven stars he's reminding the pastor that He is holding him up. By telling him He is walking among the seven lampstands, it's a reminder that the only reason the church is thriving is because of the life-giving power of Jesus.

It's a reminder of His authority and power and it is written in such a way as to eliminate any and all rebuttal about what they are about to read in the letter. He then goes right into the affirmation. He tells them that He knows they have been working hard for His Kingdom. We see that in verse 2 when He says, *"I know your deeds, your hard work and your perseverance."* He lets them know right up front that He has seen it all. He has seen their hard work, their affliction, and their perseverance. We know there was affliction because without affliction there would be no need for perseverance. Remember this was the community that ran the Apostle Paul out of town; therefore we can gain a perspective of what they were overcoming. Jesus affirms them for not giving up when they felt like it.

The fact that He affirms them for their hard work tells me that 20 percent of the people were not doing 80 percent of the work. People were serving God in this church and God himself was saying, "Good job." If you ever wonder if God sees your efforts, let this be an encouragement to you. God sees everything!

He encourages them and tells them He knows they cannot tolerate wicked men who have come out of the occult. He affirms them for testing the spirits of those who claim to be apostles, but are not, as seen in verse 2: "*I know that you cannot tolerate wicked men, that you have tested those who claim to be apostles but are not, and have found them false.*" Remember, the Apostle Paul had warned them about savage wolves that would try to infiltrate the congregation from the outside and from within, and right here we see that this body of elders took his warning to heart. They listened, rose up, and protected their front door from deadly parasites. If someone wanted to teach in their church, the elders listened closely to their doctrine and tested their gospel to ensure it was pure. They were diligent, obedient, and faithful to the instructions of Paul.

"Good job," was the word of the Lord. Good job for their perseverance and enduring hardships in Jesus' name. I am convinced they faced persecution when they called someone an evildoer or heretic. It would be natural. I am persuaded they dealt with bad press when the silversmiths talked badly about those who were affecting their business profits. Yet, God said, "Good job," not only for being theologically pure, but also for being a hardworking church. Their doctrine was right on the money, their efforts were about serving the Lord, and with that God was pleased.

## The rebuke

Now if you were the pastor you might be feeling pretty good about now, wouldn't you? You might be thinking the sought-after words we all long to hear were right around the corner. For me those words would be "Well done, thou good and faithful servant." But without missing a beat, Jesus moves right into the rebuke in verse 4 by saying, *"Yet I hold this against you: You have forsaken your first love."*

The NKJV says it best, *"You have left your first love."* It's right here where we see that while the Church of Ephesus had protected their front door, they had left their back door wide open. By concentrating so hard on theology they had forsaken their first love and had become vulnerable to a parasite.

I don't know if it really happened this way or not, but I like to imagine that the pastor was reading this letter to his congregation. In the opening affirmation I can imagine the nods and smiles, maybe even a few high fives across the pews. Perhaps their pride had been inflated a bit by the praise, but as the Lord speaks through the letter and says, *"You have forsaken your first love,"* I can only imagine a hush falling across the building as the wind in their sails vanishes. Where there might have been words of joy only moments before, now you could hear a pin drop.

What on earth does it mean to have lost their first love? What did it mean for them and what does it mean for you and me? I'm sure the pastor was scratching his head as questions ran through his mind like a ticker tape, and I imagine him wiping his brow as beads of sweat from worry formed there.

Then, as though the Lord sees the questions dancing in the minds of the pastor and congregation, He prompts their memory by saying, *"Remember the height from which you have fallen!"* I can only imagine the pastor asking himself . . . "Where have I fallen from? Where have we fallen from?"

We can find out by looking at Ephesians 1:15-17. The Book of Ephesians was the book Paul wrote to the Church of Ephesus. Remember the Book of Ephesians was written about thirty years prior to the letter to the Church of Ephesus. By looking at this passage in Ephesians, Chapter 1, we can gain greater insight into how they had fallen.

> *15For this reason, ever since I heard about your faith in the Lord Jesus and your love for all the saints, 16I have not stopped giving thanks for you, remembering you in my prayers. 17I keep asking that the God of our Lord Jesus Christ, the glorious Father, may give you the Spirit of wisdom and revelation, so that you may know him better.*

What do we see here? We see a body of individual believers who had three things going for them. The Church of Ephesus thirty years prior had a deep love and devotion for Jesus Christ himself. They were fully devoted to Jesus and had a very strong faith in Him. They trusted Him because they knew Him, intimately and individually. They also had a love that manifested itself in the way they treated and fellowshiped with other believers. I want to suggest that they had a passionate love for the Word of God and we know that because it was how they drew close to God and each other.

Their love for God and each other was so intense Scripture records here in the Book of Ephesians that Paul says he can't stop thanking God or praying for them. Paul was so taken by their relationship with Christ that he puts it in writing for all eternity. What an example this church was setting in their community. I am sure the church reached out to those in need, they helped those who were trying to take a stand against idolatry, and they loved everyone who came into their fellowship.

So what happened? It seems that in the course of the thirty years between Paul's epistle and this letter from Jesus in Revelation, a new generation of believers had been born and was growing up in the body, and over time their love for the Lord—their agape love for the Lord—had begun to cool; the passion had started to fade.

Jesus is saying to them, *"Remember the height from which you have fallen."* In this letter we see that He is specifically addressing that prior generation, the older generation. Yes, He was talking to all of them, but he was specifically addressing the generation that had something to remember. The generation that remembered the first letter from Paul affirming them for their love and devotion for God, expressed through their love and devotion for each other, and his prayerful desire for their relationship to grow— *"...so that you may know him better"* (Ephesians 1:17).

It's important to clarify here it wasn't that the Church of Ephesus had stopped loving God. They simply had stopped loving God above all. Their passion and fire for the Lord had begun to cool and, as a result, had left them vulnerable. When their hearts began cooling, other interests began to take first place.

It's a pattern in Scripture we see over and over again. Whenever a heart that was once on fire for God begins to cool, you'll see a love of things, other people, and/or activities will replace a love for God and the things of God. Ultimately, that creates an atmosphere of compromise that, if not rooted out, in time gives way to parasites that kill, steal, and destroy our first love. The Lord showed me that the cooling of our hearts puts us on the road to spiritual apathy, a dangerous and deadly condition. When our hearts begin to cool we have begun our descent into laziness, lethargy, and/or legalism.

The Lord revealed to me that the Church of Ephesus had allowed the parasite of busyness to dim their lampstand. Busyness can have a lot of faces in your life and in mine. For this body of believers, they had become so focused on their theology and fighting off the occult and idol worshipers they had lost their first love. This church got busy guarding their front doors by a continuous examination of their theology. Sadly, they forgot *why* they were doing *what* they were doing in the first place.

As they were crying, "Heretic!" they neglected to love that person to Jesus. I'm so thankful for those who have come alongside of me as I am learning to preach, teach, and write about God's Word. I'm so thankful that many who could have given up on me didn't, but loved me enough to teach me—who loved God enough to see He was using this doe-eyed girl. But I have to ask, what about you?

Is there any possibility you have been so busy serving on this board or that committee that you, too, have neglected your first love? It's easy to do. It's easy to get lost. It's easy to get so busy you lose your way. We can get so busy serving God that we forget to love God. It happens in the church, it happens on our jobs, and it happens in our homes. Without realizing it we can get so busy cleaning our houses that we turn them into idols. We can get so busy running our companies that we forget the mission we started the business for in the first place. We can get so busy serving God that we forget it's our love, praise, and devotion He truly desires the most.

It's human nature to defend ourselves when faced with the truth. We'll say, "But God, I'm doing it for you." We'll say, "But who will do it if we don't; after all, a church must have praise and worship—or Sunday school teachers or youth workers or choir members—right?" Yet, God who knows the inner rhythms of our hearts will reply, "Are you really doing it for Me? Are you sure it's not your search for significance, your desire for more money, your need to be needed that's driving you?"

I'll never forget when God showed me this particular parasite in my own life. This parasite snuck in a back door when my passion to share all I was learning stole my time away from sitting at God's feet and listening and loving Him. It took God shaking me violently before I woke up to the truth, and between you and me, this is one I still must guard against. It's my very nature to be busy, to be productive, and as a result I have to make a conscious decision to spend time simply loving Jesus and allowing Him to love me. Now, please hear my heart here; productivity is a good thing, but not when it comes at the cost of sacrificing your first love.

If it happened to them, it can happen to you. You see, anything that we allow to steal our time from sitting at His feet is a big deal to God. Anything that takes first place in our lives, other than Him, is an idol. It's as sinful and displeasing to the Lord as an idol made of silver or gold. It's a parasite.

While writing this book, I took a day off and went to the beach with some of my girlfriends. We live on the Gulf Coast of Florida and we try to get to the beach at least once a month for some R and R and, of course, a good tan. While there we observed two young mothers who were lounging near the water in front of us. One of them had five small children. They seemed to range in age from about two to six years old. As the day went on, we observed that these women were somewhat frustrated and overwhelmed by their responsibilities as mothers. As a mother of four children I can relate. We were there for an all-day beach outing and, as such, tried to befriend these ladies who weren't overly excited with the prospect of being our buddies. They seemed to prefer nurturing their own conversations and the small bottles of alcohol they were adding to their soft drinks.

As the day went on we noticed more and more small bottles were being consumed. At one point in the afternoon, all of us girls were out in the water and we casually observed that they, too, were in the water blossoming under the attention they were receiving from some attractive young men. While they were being entertained, their small children were playing in the water near the shore. The children would run back and forth from the sand to the water's edge, playing and laughing, throwing seashells at one another, and simply having a good time. Yet there was one problem; they were alone, dangerously alone without any adult supervision at all. This went on for some time and, after returning to our chairs, we noticed these children were getting burned in the hot Florida sun. Their skin was very, very pink and they were beginning to tire and get thirsty.

Two of the children had thrown sand at each other and were now rubbing their eyes, with sandy fingers, in pain. All during this time, their mothers never looked up once. They were busy frolicking with the young men and simply didn't notice what was happening with their youngsters. They kept on with the busyness of their activities, unaware of the dangers to their children. So we stepped in and cared for those sweet babies. We gave them juice boxes and washed their hands and feet with bottled water. We invited them to sit with us under our umbrellas and protected them from the sun.

I'll tell you the truth, the more we cared for those children, the angrier I got at their mommas. In fact, I was so angry I wanted to fuss at them and scold them for their irresponsibility. But in the way only He can, the Lord spoke to my heart and repeated the question, "What would love do?" He prompted me in my spirit by asking, "What would I do if I were there?" I knew what God would do: exactly what we were doing, only without anger or judgment.

I watched as their mommas finally came out of the ocean and sat down in their chairs to dry off. Immediately their children ran to them. I watched as they greeted their babies warmly. They hugged them like they had been on a long trip. They kissed them and cuddled them and smiled at them. The children responded in kind and it was in that moment I realized it wasn't that these mommas didn't love their babies. It was that for a moment, for a few minutes of innocent flirtation, they were distracted and they had neglected their first love. They were distracted by the alcohol that, for just a little while, took the heaviness of their burdens away. They were distracted by the men who, for a little while, made them feel young, carefree, and beautiful again. God wouldn't allow me to rebuke them because He had allowed me to see what so easily can happen to any of us. Stuff, things, and people can dull our sensitivity to the Spirit of God and we, in turn, can allow the parasite of busyness to dim our relationship and effectiveness for the Lord.

Friends, do you realize how blessed we are? Do you realize even on the days when we forget our first love God is still passionately pursuing us? That's the reason He wrote this letter to the Church of Ephesus. It was to bring them back to himself. It doesn't matter who or what name is on the thing drawing you away, if it has a place in your heart larger than the place Jesus holds, it's a parasite. Remember our definition of parasites—they never sit still; they feed off of the host claiming more and more territory and doing more and more damage. The longer they go undetected, the more damage they can do.

Yes, Jesus rebuked the Church of Ephesus. He rebuked

them because the parasite of busyness is a very big deal to Him. It was also a sin deal and we know that because in verse 5 Jesus tells them to repent:

> *"Repent and do the things you did at first. If you do not repent, I will come to you and remove your lamp stand from its place."*

## The Beginning of Direction

Now that Jesus has the attention of the angel of Ephesus, who, again, scholars believe to be the pastor, he gives him three sets of instructions. The first we have already covered: Jesus told the pastor and the Body of Christ to *remember*—remember what the relationship used to be like when it was new and fresh and full of fire and passion. Secondly, Jesus tells them to *repent*—meaning fall on your face and truly have a "come to Jesus" change of heart. Third, Jesus tells them to *return to* the things they did at the beginning of their relationship.

Beloved, the first step to correct any departure from God is to always go back to the place where you left Him. That same formula will work in every area of your life. If you have found yourself in a place where you still love God, but have lost that first passion, then these three steps are tangible actions you can begin today.

## Consequences

But just like the Church in Ephesus, if you do not remember, repent, and return, there will be consequences. Look at the end of verse 5: Jesus says, *"If you do not repent, I will . . . remove your lampstand from its place."*

Commentators and Bible scholars interpret this passage to mean that the church would lose its effectiveness, or in more common terms, its light would go out. But I have to wonder if that also has a deeper meaning, a meaning of much greater eternal significance. When a light goes out in a church it's because the light has gone out in the body of individual believers and as a result the light goes out in the community in which they are called to serve. The light is Jesus Christ living on the inside of us. To have their light go out means that at some point their faith has come to an end. The warning here from the Lord is stern. He tells them He is about to take action in their lives and that they are not going to like the results—eternally.

Jesus then concludes His letter with the bottom layer of Oreo and says in essence, "You can do this, as evidenced from the fact that *"You hate the practices of the Nicolaitans,"* who were a sect whose leaders thought themselves more important than the people they were supposed to be serving. They were legalistic and ruled with an iron fist and the law was their first consideration. He was counseling the Church of Ephesus to love, love, love! Love Him and then as an outward manifestation of that love, show love to others.

He wraps it up by speaking to each individual person and says, *"He who has ear, let him hear what the spirit says . . ."* In other words, He will bless those who overcome in this area with the privilege of eating at His table for all eternity! One can only ascertain that to mean if we do not overcome we may not spend eternity dining at the table of the Lord.

There is a very popular theological belief that once you accept the Lord Jesus Christ as your personal Savior you are eternally sealed until Resurrection day. Yet, I know many a believer who once gave their heart to the Lord only to take it back some time later. Having a relationship with Jesus is a daily adventure. Giving our hearts to Him isn't a one-time event. It's a one-time event we repeat day after day after day. Am I suggesting that one day of busyness can cause our lamps to go out? No. What I am suggesting is that repeatedly giving lip service to our Lord while serving other gods can.

Praise the Lord we can overcome, but we have to do so by returning to our first love! It's only by ensuring Jesus is our first love that we truly have the ability to dine with Him for all eternity. That tells me that while we cannot ever earn our salvation, we must ensure we choose Jesus first every day. Is Jesus first in your life? When was the last time you spent time curled up at His feet just sharing with Him how much you adore Him? Do you walk out that love relationship daily? Can others see Him manifested in your life?

Take the time now to put this book down and ask God to show you what He sees. Ask Him to show you your own heart. If what He sees is beautiful, great; but if not, *"remember, repent, and return"* to Him.

# 8

# Smyrna

If we were going on a journey, we would travel about thirty-five miles north of Ephesus to the Church of Smyrna in Asia Minor. Smyrna—the second letter to the second angel of the second church in the Book of Revelation. Let's take a look at it in Revelation 2:8-11:

*⁸To the angel of the church in Smyrna write:*

*These are the words of him who is the First and the Last, who died and came to life again. ⁹I know your afflictions and your poverty—yet you are rich! I know the slander of those who say they are Jews and are not, but are a synagogue of Satan.*

*¹⁰Do not be afraid of what you are about to suffer. I tell you, the devil will put some of you in prison to test you, and you will suffer persecution for ten days. Be faithful, even to the point of death, and I will give you the crown of life.*

*¹¹He who has an ear, let him hear what the Spirit says to the churches. He who overcomes will not be hurt at all by the second death.*

Smyrna was a large seaport/trading center that often competed with Ephesus for commerce. It was a beautiful and brilliant city with wide, paved streets and ornately structured architecture. It was known throughout the region for its fine schools of science and medicine. As you might have guessed, it was also a wealthy city supported by the leadership of the Roman emperor. The government gave freely to enterprises in this city because the political and prominent business leaders of Smyrna were fully loyal to Rome, endorsing their policies and decisions. However, the Church of Smyrna did not support Rome the way it was expected, and as a result their lack of political loyalty caused the church great heartache and persecution.

The church had two main problems. First of all, it was located in the midst of a Jewish population that was strongly opposed to Christianity. Secondly, the city itself was so loyal to Rome it supported emperor worship. We see evidence of both in Jesus' letter to the Church of Smyrna in verse 9 of this chapter.

Jesus begins by saying, *"I know your afflictions* (meaning tribulations and burdens) *and your poverty."* Your afflictions and your poverty? I find it odd that Jesus would call this church afflicted and in poverty when there was so much wealth around it. Yet, that is exactly what it was. It was checkbook poor, can't go to the grocery store poor, bankrupt poor. We know this because the word poverty in verse 9— *ptocheian*—is a word that means poor to the point of begging.

I'll tell you the truth; that puzzled me. Why would a church that was made up of citizens of the Smyrna community allow their church to be in a poverty state? I wondered about it. I wondered if only poor people attended the church. I wondered if the church was attended by non-tithers. I wondered if the church was inadequately attended. But after reading commentator after commentator, I discovered the church was poor to the point of begging because the Roman government regularly plundered and stole from the Christians. Remember that a congregation is made of people within a community. So when a church is in poverty, it's likely that the people who make up the church are living in poverty.

That's exactly what was happening in Smyrna. They were being afflicted with poverty. You see, the Christians who made up the Church of Smyrna were being raped and robbed of all of their tangible wealth by the Roman government. Because they wouldn't give freely and legally, their wealth was being stolen. And yet right there in verse 9 Jesus tells them, "I know about your situation and I want you to know you are rich." Rich—a word that means abounding, overflowing with riches: eternal riches—being stored up in Heaven where thieves cannot break in and steal (see Matthew 6:20). That ought to be comforting to anyone who is being persecuted by someone else's heavy hand. You may feel like you're being raked over the coals and robbed of earthly blessings, but God says you are rich!

Rome was having its way and Jesus acknowledges that. But Smyrna was also having another problem. Look at verse 9. Here we see the other source of affliction. The slander of those who say they are Jews but are not. Who were these people who proclaimed to be Jews? We find a very precise definition of a real Jew in Romans 2:28-29:

> 28A man is not a Jew if he is only one outwardly, nor is circumcision merely outward and physical. 29No, a man is a Jew if he is one inwardly; and circumcision is circumcision of the heart, by the Spirit, not by the written code. Such a man's praise is not from men, but from God.

From this passage we can determine these were people

who were born Jews, but had not been circumcised in their hearts. That means they had not accepted Jesus as their Savior. They were only Jews by birth, yet the pride of their heritage had blinded them to their true spiritual condition. If you have accepted Jesus as Lord and Savior, demonstrated by the spiritual fruit being produced in your life, you are truly saved. However, these Jews from birth were nominal Christians only.

Now, if Jesus in His letter had just stopped there and said the Church of Smyrna was being slandered by unbelievers, it might be bad enough, but He goes even further and says the Church of Smyrna was being afflicted, tormented, and slandered by a synagogue of Satan. Friends, the Church of Smyrna was being tormented by followers of Satan. This is a hard thing to deal with because no one, and I do mean no one, is pleased when their faith is challenged. Thank goodness I don't have to be the one to challenge them. Jesus is doing it for me in verse 9. The Lord himself says the Church of Smyrna was being afflicted and robbed by those who "*say they are Jews and are not.* " As a result of not recognizing their hearts did not truly belong to the Lord, they were being used by Satan to persecute, torment, martyr, and murder true Christians.

Several weeks ago, my girlfriends and I spent the day at the Holy Land Experience in Orlando, Florida. If you've never been there, think "Israel meets Disney World" and you will understand. While we were there we attended The Passion Play, which depicted Jesus' death.

One particular scene captured my attention. Picture Jesus being whipped and tortured and then spat on and slandered as He carries His Cross to Calvary. Now picture Satan dressed in black walking alongside of Him. Do you see it? As Jesus was walking along, struggling to carry His Cross, the

Roman soldiers were mocking Him. They were calling Him such ugly names even the strongest in the audience cringed. Yet I noticed that every time a Roman soldier spoke, Satan's mouth was moving. It only took a few sentences for me to realize that Satan was influencing the guards in what they were saying. It wasn't Satan telling the guard what to say and the guard repeating it. No, in fact Satan and the guard were speaking at the exact same time. They were in one accord; they were one.

In the Church of Smyrna, these Jews were so proud of their heritage that they looked down on the Smyrnean church. They were not acting in love, they were acting in judgment and their pride blinded them to the truth—the truth that they were being used as Satan's pawns.

History indicates that millions of Christian Smyrneans were martyred for their faith during biblical times. Smyrna was governed by Rome and the Romans liked to be entertained, so they built a huge coliseum in the city to house sporting events. One of those sporting events was called "Feed the Christians to the lions." Another was called "Burn the Christians at the stake." Yet, in spite of the millions who were being martyred for their faith, or perhaps as a result of it, the Church of Smyrna thrived. It grew, and more and more people came to know the Lord.

## Double Stuff of Love and Encouragement

Remember Jesus has an amazing way of communicating with us and, as stated before, I call His method the Oreo cookie mode because there is usually an affirmation, followed by a rebuke, and then guidance and direction. However, for the Church of Smyrna, Jesus mixes it up. He still uses the Oreo cookie technique, but this time instead of a rebuke, He delivers a double stuff of encouragement and love to His people, described in verse 10:

*Do not be afraid of what you are about to suffer. I tell you, the devil will put some of you in prison to test you, and you will suffer persecution for ten days. Be faithful, even to the point of death, and I will give you the crown of life.*

Now, without a rebuke, we might be tempted to believe that there was no parasite living among the members of the Church of Smyrna, and initially that may seem to be the case. Ah, but Jesus. . . . After thoughtful prayer and consideration, He revealed to me that there were two parasites ever-present, looking and waiting for an opportunity to sneak through a back door. Look again at verse 10:

*Do not be afraid* . . . Jesus told them that for ten days, which biblically speaking it is believed to mean ten years (see Numbers 14:34 and Ezekiel 4:6), they were going to suffer, go to prison, and be put to death. If the Lord just told you what He just told them, what would you be feeling?

I don't know about you but I would be feeling fear—full-out fear, shaking in my boots fear, ready to high-tail it out of Dodge, moving south or north kind of fear. Ever present, looking for a place to sneak in through their back door was the parasite of fear.

Fear—this emotion can significantly diminish or even kill our effectiveness for the Kingdom of God. Fear—the kind that makes our tongues swell up so that we can't share our testimony. Fear—that produces the *fight or flight* reaction when all God really wants us for us to do is stand strong.

And yet here we find Jesus telling them, *"Do not be afraid . . . "* Do not let the parasite of fear begin to diminish your light or your testimony. A little bit further along Jesus told them to be faithful, even to the point of death. That verse reveals to me a second parasite that was hovering, the parasite of compromise. Instead of illustrating what the parasite of compromise is, here is a brief overview of what it isn't, according to one scholar:

> *One of the people who suffered the most was a pastor of the Smyrna church. His name was Polycarp. Polycarp was eighty-six years old when he died for his faith in Jesus Christ. He was the pastor of the church of Smyrna, ordained by the Apostle John and had faithfully pastored the people of Smyrna for forty years. The Romans came to get him one Friday night and he was murdered the very next day on the Sabbath, February 23, 155 AD. On the night he was arrested he asked the Romans as they entered his home if they were hungry. Answering, "Yes," he replied, "Let me have a meal cooked for you." So there while the Romans enjoyed the meal he had prepared, Polycarp spent his last hour in prayer. Then they took him. They took him to the great amphitheater where he met the governor. Governor Status Quadratus was his name. History tells us that the Governor was impressed with Polycarp. So impressed that he desired to let Polycarp go free. So he said to him, "Polycarp, all you have to do to save your life is just curse Christ. That's all. Curse Christ and we won't do anything to you." Polycarp said, "Eighty-six years I have served Him, and He never once wronged me. How then shall I blaspheme my King who has saved me?"*

No wonder the Smyrneans were so strong in their faith. They were led by a true man of God.

*History report in* The Martyrdom of Polycarp (Kirsopp Lake translation) *that as Polycarp entered the arena he heard a voice from Heaven saying: "Be strong." And he was strong. The crowd in the arena shouted for him to be fed to the lions but they were already full from eating other Christians and they showed no interest in Polycarp. Some other people shouted, "Let's burn him at the stake." So, even though it was the Sabbath they made the fire ready mocking him for the good that Christians believed in. As they were about to bind him to the stake Polycarp said, "Please don't tie me up. He who gives me the power to endure the fire will also grant me the strength to remain in the flame." And so they didn't tie him up, and he stood there. As they lit the fire we're told in various history books that the flames parted around him like a tent. And he was protected. Finally the authorities had to thrust him through with their spears killing him.*

Polycarp didn't back down in his faith when the flames got hot. But if we aren't careful, when the heat of living the Christian life gets too intense, we will be tempted to compromise our faith out of fear and put out the lamp of the one who lives in us.

## The Victor's Crown

I want you to notice this was no *Health, Wealth and Prosperity* letter. There was no promise that Jesus would deliver them from the hands of the Romans while they were on Earth. There isn't always a happily ever after on Earth. Sometimes the good guy loses, sometimes bad things happen to good people, and sometimes Satan wins a battle. But for those who believe, he never wins the war. For those who are faithful God promises to provide the crown of life.

In the Bible you will find three different meanings for the word *crown*. There is the *diadem crown* or better known as the *royal crown*. There is the *crown of pain* or better known as the *crown of thorns*. And then there is the crown that Jesus is referring to in verse 10. This crown is called the *victor's crown*.

The victor's crown is a crown made of olive branches, laurel, evergreen, and celery. Physically speaking, it was a crown often given to contestants who had participated in games and had victoriously crossed the finish line. Spiritually speaking, it is a crown awarded to those receiving eternal life. Jesus in His great love and mercy promises the Church of Smyrna that if they will overcome the desire to compromise their faith out of fear, He will know they are truly His disciples and will grant them eternal life.

Bible teacher Nancy Leigh DeMoss said it best when she said, "The only way to avoid suffering for your faith is to compromise it; to fear man rather than God."

The truth is, we all want to be liked. We all want to be applauded and recognized. No one likes to be made fun of. But to what end are we willing to gain another's approval? I want to encourage you to take stock of your life right now as this chapter comes to a close. Is there any possibility you are compromising your faith out of fear? Could it be if you don't go out drinking with your buddies you're afraid you'll be called a goody-goody? Is there any possibility you've taken your Bible off your desk because your boss made a sarcastic comment about it? Is there any chance you've stopped pursuing your calling because it might cost you a relationship?

I don't know what you're dealing with, but I know what I've had to deal with. I remember when a good friend at the time said, "Tina, it'll be okay if you never get to fulfill the dreams of your heart." I remember she said it during a time when my husband wasn't pleased that I was serving the Lord in the way in which He had called me. The first time, I failed the faith test and gave in to fear. The second time, I shook in my boots. The third time, I stood my ground and it cost me a great price.

You need to know there are times that serving God will cost you plenty. Thankfully, at least in America, Christians are no longer fed to lions, but I know some people that would give the king of the jungle a run for their money. This I know for sure, if you will take a stand against the fear in your life, God will empower you to endure the hardships.

Right now wherever you are, I invite you to lift both hands to the Lord and in a tangible act of surrender release that fear to your heavenly Father. I promise you on the authority of the Word of God, if you will surrender, He will empower you to stand.

I close with this Scripture and pray you will be encouraged by it:

> *"Hear me, you who know what is right, you people who have my law in your hearts: Do not fear the reproach of men or be terrified by their insults. For the moth will eat them up like a garment; the worm will devour them like wool. But my righteousness will last forever, my salvation through all generations"* (Isaiah 51:7-8).

# 9

# Pergamum

Today we take a look at the third letter to the third angel of the third church: the Church of Pergamum. If you read from The King James Version you'll see that the Church of Pergamum is called the Church of Pergamos. Same church, just a different way of saying the name.

The letter to this church is found in Revelation 2:12-17:

> *¹²To the angel of the church in Pergamum write: sThese are the words of him who has the sharp, double-edged sword. ¹³I know where you live—where Satan has his throne. Yet you remain true to my name. You did not renounce your faith in me, even in the days of Antipas, my faithful witness, who was put to death in your city—where Satan lives.*

> *¹⁴Nevertheless, I have a few things against you: You have people there who hold to the teaching of Balaam, who taught Balak to entice the Israelites to sin by eating food sacrificed to idols and by committing sexual immorality. ¹⁵Likewise you also have those who hold to the teaching of the Nicolaitans. ¹⁶Repent therefore!*

*Otherwise, I will soon come to you and will fight against them with the sword of my mouth.*

*[17] He who has an ear, let him hear what the Spirit says to the churches. To him who overcomes, I will give some of the hidden manna. I will also give him a white stone with a new name written on it, known only to him who receives it.*

This has been the most complicated letter to read and teach so far, but I pray by the power of the Holy Spirit that God will make His Word known. A bit of context is needed here, so we will first look at the city of Pergamum.

Pergamum was about fifty-five miles north of Smyrna and it sat high on a hill surrounded by beautiful countryside. It was a wealthy, sophisticated, materialistic city that was the center of Greek culture and education, housing a library of over 200,000 books. It doesn't sound like a lot until you take into account that printing and copying didn't exist at that time. Every one of those books was written by hand.

It is also important to note that Pergamum was the capital city of the Roman province of Asia. Additionally, because it was the Greek epicenter of culture, the city was filled with architecturally impressive buildings and statues of many Greek gods and goddesses such as Zeus and Athena. All of these factors made Pergamum a very dangerous place to live if you were a Christian, and especially if you participated in Christian worship.

Because it was the capital city, many Roman officials lived there including the Roman Caesars. They demanded to be worshiped as gods, and because Greek culture was so widespread, the city leaders expected everyone to worship the statues as if they were idols. Can you imagine walking down the street and being expected to bow every time you encountered a politician or a statue? That was the environment of the day. That was Pergamum.

While most commentators believe there were four main cults in the city of Pergamum, people came from all around the world to worship one main god called *Asklepios*. It was a pagan god in the form of a serpent believed to be the god of healing. Even in the first century Church the greatest need of the city was to be healed of disease and the people of Pergamum believed that Asklepios could heal them.

From a godly perspective, this was not a nice city. In fact, looking again at verse 13, Jesus tells the Church of Pergamos, *"I know where you live—you live where Satan has his throne."*

## The Church of Pergamum

It's interesting to note if you look at this Scripture in the NKJV, it would read, *"I know . . . where you dwell."* Dwell, a word that means to take up residence; however, it's a place where you lay your head, but not your heart. The Lord wanted them to know they were doing a great job of living in the world but not responding to or acting as though they were a part of it.

I was having an impassioned conversation with someone a while back about priorities and life here on Earth, and I said, "This is not my home; this is just where I live." You see in that conversation I wanted it known that the things of this world will never be as important to me as the things of God.

That is what's meant here in part, but it's also spoken from what appears to be a knowing place of compassion. A place where Jesus might say, "Look, I know where you are and what you're dealing with." For those of us who might be tempted to think God can't see us or doesn't seem to care about what we're going through, we need to remember that God's Word is the same yesterday, today, and forever. Our

Pergamum might be the world we live in, or the community, or the workplace, or our marriage, or family, but God says, "I get it, I see, I know."

We know because continuing in verse 13, Jesus gives them the first layer of the Oreo cookie by affirming their faith in His name. He affirms and compliments them for remaining true to Him, even when a man by the name of Antipas is martyred. The Lord affirms them for their loyalty. But His affirmation is short-lived because in verse 14, we very quickly see that He has a double stuff rebuke for this church.

**The Rebuke**

Look at verses 14 and 15:

> *14Nevertheless, I have a few things against you: You have people there who hold to the teaching of Balaam, who taught Balak to entice the Israelites to sin by eating food sacrificed to idols and by committing sexual immorality. 15Likewise you also have those who hold to the teaching of the Nicolaitans.*

Jesus begins His rebuke by telling them they have people teaching a Balaam doctrine. If you are not familiar with this story, here is a quick overview and you can read about it in Numbers 22.

Balaam was a prophet who dabbled on both sides of the fence. He appears to serve both God and Satan. Numbers 22 tells us a king named Balak was afraid of the Israelites so he wanted Balaam to put a curse on them. Balaam, however, heard from the Lord and after a few God-encounters, which included a talking donkey, Balaam tells Balak he can't help him. However, later in the Book of Numbers, you'll find that Balaam compromises his faith and gives in to Balak in a sneaky, underhanded way. He knows he cannot curse the Israelites, so instead he tells King Balak how to corrupt them. He encourages King Balak to send his women into the Israelites' camp to entice the men. The men end up easy prey and ultimately are not only having sexual relations with the women of this land, but are also marrying them and worshiping their idols, as well as the Most High God.

What Balaam hosted in his body was the worm of compromise. You see, it's clear that Satan couldn't curse the Israelites because God's mighty hand of protection was upon them. Instead he decided to corrupt them through the parasite of compromise. This devilish worm whispered in their ears, "You can have that woman and still be married to your Israelite wife." He whispered in their ears, "You can worship the goddess of Athena and your Jehovah Jirah." Does the old saying, "Liar, liar pants on fire" come to mind? Because that's who the enemy is: a big fat compromising liar!

He does the same with you and me every day. Satan knows where we live. He knows we live in a world that is busy, chaotic, and sinful. He knows that technology is free and anger is cheap. So when God gives him a big *No* on the curse card, he redirects his attention to luring us to compromise. He uses anything and everything that is even remotely one of our weaknesses and encourages us to do it.

Think back to the Church of Ephesus and remember that he'll invite us to get busy instead of spending time with God. He'll create fear in our hearts like he tried to do in Smyrna and get us to compromise our faith in the Word of the Lord. He'll create the opportunity for us to get angry with our spouse and rob us of the hope and faith in our vows. He'll entice us with the things and people of this world that are not good for us, and tell us it's okay because we still sing in the choir or serve in a ministry.

Satan is subtle and because God originally created him as an angel, he's also smart. So when he isn't allowed to attack from the front he'll sneak in where we're weak, vulnerable, and irritable. Is there someone in your life—man, woman or child—who gets on your nerves? If you have anything in your heart for them other than the love of our Father, it's a snare. Is there an area of temptation that you continually seem to battle? If so, that's a gift from God to warn you that you need to be completely on guard because it's a snare. You see, we can't even dabble in sin; not even a little.

Holding a grudge is a sin. Acting on your anger is a sin. Feeling proud is a sin. Judging other people's actions is a sin. We can't even toy with them because inevitably, a dabble will turn into a drizzle which will turn into downpour that results in a draining of God's anointing and a drowning of God's Spirit.

The spirit of compromise was all over Pergamum and by the looks of Jesus' letter, He was not happy with them. If I were the pastor reading this letter, I'd be about to lead my congregation in an altar call. But Jesus doesn't stop there. He continues to rebuke them for holding on to the teachings of the Nicolaitans, who believed you could hold to the truths of God's Word *and* enjoy the sinful pleasures the world had to offer. Again we see the parasite of compromise.

We've seen how parasites grow in the body. They move into one cell and then they look for weaknesses in another before they make their move and multiply. Compromise is the same way. I can say, "I will not, ever, ever have an affair," but if I allow the parasite of lust to enter into my heart, then it's truly only a matter of time before one gives way to the other.

You might say, "Not me," but think about King David who was called "a man after God's own heart"—and still he strayed. I can say, "I will never murder anyone," but if I allow anger and resentment and bitterness to invade my soul, it is only a matter of time before that which is in my heart flows out of my mouth and kills someone's spirit.

Compromise; it's an ugly, ugly parasite that was living off of this church. We have a responsibility to find out if it's living in us. Please don't think for a second you know already because the Bible says our hearts have the capacity to deceive us. We need to ask God. If we find it is there, in any area, we need to follow the advice in verse 16:

*"Repent therefore!"*

Two words! No mealy-mouthing about it. I might follow that up with "Do it!" Today. Now. Don't wait. Because Jesus quickly says, if you do not, I will come to you and fight you with the sword of my mouth. He's not talking to the city of Pergamum here. He's talking to the Church. He's talking to you and he's talking to me.

## The Sword of God's Mouth

The sword of God's mouth refers to judgment: swift, fierce, earthly, and eternal judgment. Jesus makes it really clear here that we, as the Body of Christ, must remain pure at all costs and separate ourselves from any form of compromise. Let me be clear. Jesus is not asking for perfection here. I believe He's asking for intention.

Intentional living. Intentional choices. Intentional searching and intentional repentance. And to those who overcome . . . He'll give some of the hidden manna. Hidden manna is spiritual food: strength, wisdom, insight, and provision. Hidden because only Jesus knows where it is: manna which rains from that heavenly hiding place. The Scripture here promises to give us what we need if only we will not compromise.

Jesus also promises to give the Church of Pergamum (and us) a white stone, declaring it acquitted, guilt-free, and redeemed. In Bible days whenever a person was on trial, the jury would be given two stones: a white one for innocence and a black one for guilt. Based upon the verdict, the jury would take the appropriate stone and place it before the accused or throw it on the ground in front of them to indicate the way they judged the crime. So, for Jesus to say He'll give you a white stone, it means you've been found clean, innocent, and redeemed by the blood of the Lamb. You'll not just be clean; you'll be pure.

Then, if that weren't enough, the Lord says He'll give you a new name just like he did for me. Once upon a time I was Tina Denise Brenneman Chesnutt Blount; but now I am daughter of the Most High God. To Him, my name is Beautiful. Ask Him for yours.

He offers three gifts for those who will choose to overcome the parasite of compromise: hidden manna, a white stone, and a new name. Whatever you have to give up, do it now! It's worth it. He's worth it. Wouldn't you agree?

CHAPTER

# 10

# Thyatira

The fourth letter to the fourth angel of the fourth church in Asia Minor, the Church of Thyatira is found in Revelation 2:18-29:

> *¹⁸To the angel of the church in Thyatira write:*
>
> *These are the words of the Son of God, whose eyes are like blazing fire and whose feet are like burnished bronze. ¹⁹I know your deeds, your love and faith, your service and perseverance, and that you are now doing more than you did at first.*
>
> *²⁰Nevertheless, I have this against you: You tolerate that woman Jezebel, who calls herself a prophetess. By her teaching she misleads my servants into sexual immorality and the eating of food sacrificed to idols.*
>
> *²¹I have given her time to repent of her immorality, but she is unwilling. ²²So I will cast her on a bed of suffering, and I will make those who commit adultery with her suffer intensely, unless they repent of her ways. ²³I will strike her children dead. Then all the churches*

*will know that I am he who searches hearts and minds, and I will repay each of you according to your deeds.*

*24Now I say to the rest of you in Thyatira, to you who do not hold to her teaching and have not learned Satan's so-called deep secrets (I will not impose any other burden on you): 25Only hold on to what you have until I come.*

*26To him who overcomes and does my will to the end, I will give authority over the nations— 27'He will rule them with an iron scepter; he will dash them to pieces like pottery'— just as I have received authority from my Father. 28I will also give him the morning star.*

*29He who has an ear, let him hear what the Spirit says to the churches.*

Thyatira was located about forty miles southeast of Pergamum. If you were visiting these cities in order you would have started in Ephesus, traveled north to Smyrna, then on to Pergamum, and now you would be making a sharp right hand turn on Asia Minor Highway and would be heading due southeast. Unlike the wealthy, educated, and sophisticated city of Pergamum, Thyatira was known to be a workingman's town. It was a city that had been established by Alexander the Great and was rich in agriculture. Farmers made their living in Thyatira because it was a place where country boys could survive.

Yet, in spite of its rich soil and farmland, Thyatira was really known for being a gateway and gatekeeper to Pergamum. It was a city that was on a trade route. People came from all over Asia Minor and traveled through it to get to the larger cities. As a result of its location, this city became the setting for small trade businesses. It was known for all kinds of trading guilds such as cloth and purple dyes, leather, pottery, etc. Even secular books reveal to us that the trading guilds were Thyatira's claim to fame.

Trading guilds were like religious labor unions. Every type of trade had its own guild or union. These types of unions held regular business meetings and social activities. At these meetings the leader of the guild would require those in attendance to worship and offer sacrifices to the patron gods of whatever the trade was. The god of leather, the god of purple dye, the god of pottery . . .

These meetings and activities were held in what were called patron temples and it was expected that if you were a farmer, for example, you show up for whatever the activity was at the guild that week. But these weren't just ordinary get-togethers. These were Playboy mansion gatherings. The kind where the wine flowed freely and the prostitutes gave freely.

It was the norm in Thyatira. Everyone participated. It was accepted. It was expected—if you wanted to make a living in that town. Not participating in the guild was social and financial suicide.

## The Church of Thyatira

The Church of Thyatira was a small church located in this little trade town, which had no major cults, and yet, interestingly enough, the Lord writes the longest, strongest letter of them all to it. It is the most complex letter; one that kept me up and on my face for hours before Him, seeking His wisdom and asking for understanding for how to apply the object lesson of this church to our lives.

"Why?" I asked God. "Why was this church even noticed? Why, of all the cities where occult practices and idol worship were so blatantly formed, would you even bother with this small town?" I found His answer very, very interesting. I pray that you'll discover it as well. In verses 18 and 19, Jesus begins by affirming this church for their deeds. He lists four of them.

> [18] *"To the angel of the church in Thyatira write:*
>
> *These are the words of the Son of God, whose eyes are like blazing fire and whose feet are like burnished bronze.* [19] *I know your deeds, your love and faith, your service and perseverance, and that you are now doing more than you did at first."*

The Lord introduces himself as the Son of God with eyes that see everything and whose feet are ready to act upon what He sees. With that established, he begins the letter by affirming them for their love, their faith, their service, and their perseverance.

It's interesting to note the love He's affirming them for is *agape* love. Not *phileo* love. He's saying good job, you are loving each other unconditionally. You love each other, not as brothers, but in the way that I love you. In contrast to the Church of Ephesus, we see Jesus' love actively flowing out of them toward each other.

This was a church which had a strong faith, and not only faith lifted up, but faith in action. We know that because Jesus also affirms them for their service. Service out of love and faithfulness is a beautiful thing and they persevered doing it over time.

This was a church that genuinely cared about and took care of one another. This was also a church that was growing in its relationship with Jesus Christ. We know because Jesus affirms them for doing more than they did at first. These were true believers because they were growing in their faith. As 2 Corinthians 13:5 tells us, we need to test our faith to ensure we are saved. We as believers need to look for a growing awareness of God's presence, power, and fruit in our lives to ensure we are truly saved and not just living by head knowledge.

Thyatira was a good church with good, God-fearing people in it. But they, too, had a parasite: a very, dark, dangerous parasite. We discover it in verse 20.

> *Nevertheless, I have this against you: You tolerate that woman Jezebel, who calls herself a prophetess. By her teaching she misleads my servants into sexual immorality and the eating of food sacrificed to idols.*

This church was being eaten from the inside out by the parasite of tolerance. They were tolerating a woman called Jezebel.

## The Parasite of Tolerance

At first glance you might think, "Wow, that woman has lived for a *long* time," thinking of Jezebel in the Old Testament. But this was a woman who had a Jezebel spirit. If you read through the Book of I Kings, you'll find that Jezebel was the daughter of a king and wife of a king. History records her as being one of the most evil characters in Scripture because she served both God and Baal. We see a similar characterization in Revelation of this woman in Thyatira. This woman who calls herself a prophetess, who misleads God's servants into sexual immorality and idol worship.

To make it real for us, most scholars believe this woman taught a doctrine that communicated that it was okay for Christians to party and be sexually immoral at these trade guilds. They suggested she encouraged believers to drink freely, offer sacrifices to patron gods, and sleep with whomever they fancied. And she taught this in the church.

Sounds ridiculous, doesn't it? "Why on earth would a church put up with that?" Why wouldn't they open their Bibles and say, "Show me where that kind of thinking lines up with the Word of God?" I'd like to suggest to you this was a woman with influence, a woman who had a voice, a woman who perhaps taught some of the truth, but not all of the truth; much like the enemy does with us today. She probably made a good argument and drew on people's emotions. After all, these farmers and tradesmen had families to support.

Certainly Jesus would understand that it's just what they had to do to survive, right? This woman had an intelligent argument and people believed her. The same thing happens in churches today. Maybe it's not over drinking and sex. Maybe it's over homosexuality, abortion, tithing, the pastor, or even the building of a new church. Perhaps it's over divorce. I know of individuals in the church who appear to be spiritual pillars in the community and yet they condone divorce when one party "isn't happy." Where is the spiritual integrity there? Where is the watchman on the wall?

It's happening now in the twenty-first century Church, but make no mistake, it began in the first century Church. Any way you slice it, this woman was leading some of God's servants away from the truth. This is a blatant sin that will be addressed shortly. But first, what about the parasite? In verse 24 of this passage, it tells us there were others in the church who didn't buy into what she was selling. However, they were tolerating her and this is what Jesus was rebuking them for. He says, "*I have this against you: You tolerate that woman . . .* "

It's important to note here that not all tolerance is a sin, but when a leader or church body tolerates a person in a church who is leading others away from their faith and is contributing to the division of a church or a family, that, my friends, is sin. We know they were tolerating her because in the original language we see the church body *"sufferest that woman."* They were doing nothing about her. They were allowing her to poison them because of the parasite of tolerance! Maybe they realized they were wrong or maybe they didn't, but that doesn't change the Word of the Lord. As believers it is our responsibility to get to know God and the Word of God. Ignorance can be as deadly a parasite as tolerance.

## Why Are You Suffering?

I heard a story about a dog that was seen lying on its owner's front porch howling in pain. A passerby asked the owner, "Why is your dog howling so?" The owner replied, "Oh, he's lying on a nail." The passerby questioned, "Then why doesn't he move off of it?" "Because," the owner responded, "it must not hurt badly enough."

Why was this church suffering so? I'd like to suggest that their greatest strength (front door) had become their greatest weakness (back door). It was because of love. Remember this was a church that was affirmed for their love. The angel, or pastor, of this church loved in an agape way.

Remember the Church of Ephesus was affirmed for its commitment to pure doctrine, but were chastised for their lack of love. Here we see just the opposite. Thyatira was affirmed for its love but rebuked for allowing heresy in its midst. That tells us something really, really important—we have to have both love and truth. One without the other is potentially fatal. That is why when the Lord speaks He does so with a double-edged sword. bringing both comfort and conviction. We need to be balanced. As believers in Jesus Christ, sometimes the most loving thing we can do is to confront tolerance.

## The Consequences of Tolerance

As we are about to see, tolerating someone within the church who is leading others astray is serious business, which is why I believe Jesus included this little country church in His round of letters. Matthew 18:6 says it would be better to hang a millstone around someone's neck and drown them in the depths of the sea, than for them to cause one of God's children to sin.

Look again at verses 21-23 of chapter 2:

> *²¹I have given her time to repent of her immorality, but she is unwilling. ²²So I will cast her on a bed of suffering, and I will make those who commit adultery with her suffer intensely, unless they repent of her ways.*

> *²³I will strike her children dead. Then all the churches will know that I am he who searches hearts and minds, and I will repay each of you according to your deeds.*

I am fond of verse 21 because it is a beautiful picture of Jesus' mercy. Even though this woman was causing division in the church and leading others astray, Jesus gave her time to repent. Aren't you glad that His love for us is so great He will call us to repentance? He doesn't have to give us time, but He does. He doesn't have to give us opportunity to repent, but He does.

Many times in Scripture we are warned not to harden our hearts. Jezebel had hardened her heart and now God's judgment was about to be unleashed. Jesus begins by saying that as a result of her hardened heart, He is going to cast her on a bed of suffering. Those reading this letter will remember that the Old Testament Jezebel was thrown from her window and devoured by dogs (see 2 Kings 9:33-36). This is a warning to them of her death, and not just her earthly death but also the second, eternal death.

112

That may sound harsh, but God reminds us in Ezekiel 33 that He takes no pleasure in doing this. He begs us to repent! He desires that none of us should perish; not even one. But He's still the Lord with eyes of blazing fire who sees all and stands ready to act. He's very clear that if she does not repent she will be cast into the Lake of Fire.

Verse 22 tells us that, not only will God make her lie in the bed she made, but He also warns that those who have committed adultery with her will suffer intensely should they not repent.

These words—*commit adultery*—have duel meanings. They mean not only the sexual act, but also the spiritual one. The act that has them cheating on God by not honoring and fulfilling the true gospel, and also believing a lie that was fed to them. He's telling those true believers who were fed a lie to repent and come back to Him; otherwise they are going to suffer intensely. Suffering, as we know, is often how God brings us back to Him. We re-enter that relationship through the gate of repentance.

Jesus' voice gets stronger in verse 23 when He says, "*I will strike her children dead.*" He is not talking about Jezebel's physical children here. He's talking about those followers who have been raised up under her who don't just believe in the lie, but are now using their voices to lead others astray. The Lord literally says, "I will strike them dead"—physically dead, and perhaps, spiritually dead too. The end of verse 23 tells us He will do this so all the churches will know you can't get away with this kind of evil in His house. He reminds us in this passage that we may think we are getting away with something, but God sees all and He will eventually hold us accountable.

## God's Direction

Jesus had a need for the pastor, leaders, and saints of this church to step up. He says in verse 24 that for those who had not bought into Satan's schemes and who held on to the true faith, there would be no more burdens. True faith at times involves true biblical discipline, not tolerance.

I can't help but wonder if when the day comes that the pastor, deacon board, and church body of Thyatira meet with Jesus face-to-face, will they be told they have blood on their hands? Not for what they did do, but for what they didn't do and for the lives and souls that were lost as a result.

2 Peter 3:9 tells us the Lord is patient with us, not wanting anyone to perish, but desiring that everyone come to repentance. And should we, like the Church in Thyatira, overcome, He promises us two things: authority over the nations and the bright morning star.

Authority over the nations means we'll rule with Him in the earthly millennial kingdom. And the bright morning star is Jesus Christ himself. He promises us himself in all of His fullness. *"He who has an ear, let him hear what the Spirit says to the churches."* He's talking to us. He's talking to me and He's talking to you.

Do you hear Him?

CHAPTER

# 11

# Sardis

This is the fifth letter to the fifth angel of the fifth church in Asia Minor; the Church of Sardis in Revelation 3:1-6:

*¹To the angel of the church in Sardis write:*

*These are the words of him who holds the seven spirits of God and the seven stars. I know your deeds; you have a reputation of being alive, but you are dead. ²Wake up! Strengthen what remains and is about to die, for I have not found your deeds complete in the sight of my God.*

*³Remember, therefore, what you have received and heard; obey it, and repent. But if you do not wake up, I will come like a thief, and you will not know at what time I will come to you.*

*⁴Yet you have a few people in Sardis who have not soiled their clothes. They will walk with me, dressed in white, for they are worthy. ⁵He who overcomes will, like them, be dressed in white. I will never blot out his name from the book of life, but will acknowledge his name before my Father and his angels.*

*6He who has an ear, let him hear what the Spirit says to the churches.*

Sardis was located about fifty miles east of Smyrna and thirty miles southeast of Thyatira. We are making an upside-down "U" in direction, and right now we are headed due south. At one time, Sardis had been an important and wealthy city, known for its textile industry and the dyeing of wool. Sardis had even been the capital city of the province, however, a series of hostile invasions and a major earthquake had devastated the city and the Roman government had relocated to Pergamum.

This city was split in two locations: it had an older city and a newer one, perhaps like Tampa and New Tampa where I live. The older city was set up high on a mountain with steep cliffs on every side. Geographically, the city appeared to be almost impenetrable and this belief gave the leaders of the community a false sense of security, and as a result they had been devastated by war. So a newer section had been built. Yet in spite of the new construction, at the time of the writing of this letter, the city of Sardis was in the process of dying.

## The Church of Sardis

Jesus' letter to the Church of Sardis seems to indicate that what was true of the city was also true of the church. However, it was not only dying; it was dead. In verse 1 we see for the first time in all of these letters, there is no affirmation.

Jesus usually uses the Oreo cookie method of communication, giving an affirmation, a rebuke, and then a call to action with guidance and encouragement. This time, there is no warm, fuzzy affirmation given at all, but He gets right to the point when He says, *"I know your deeds; you have a reputation of being alive, but you are dead."*

Breaking this verse down to get a clearer picture in our heads of this church, Jesus begins by saying, *"I know your deeds.*" We can assume from this phrase that like many of the other churches we have studied, this was not an ineffective church. The pastor preached, the congregation prayed, they probably had worship, and programs—maybe even an Easter or Christmas pageant.

They were also a well-known church; we know this because the only way you get a reputation is if people are talking about you. So we assume the congregation and the community saw all of the activity in the church and said, "Wow, that's a happening church." But at the end of verse 1, Jesus makes it very clear that there is a big difference between reputation and reality, because He calls this church *dead*. Notice that in every other letter Jesus rebukes a certain sect of the church, but in this letter He rebukes the church at large. He calls them dead—the entire church, dead.

Now there are two theories as to what He means. One theory is this church was saved once upon a time, but it has become somewhat comatose. Perhaps life has taken a toll on it and as a result it has lost its zeal, its passion, and its fire. The second theory is these people from Sardis are really spiritually dead, having never accepted Jesus Christ as their personal Savior. Either way, we find that these are decent people, not involved with witchcraft, sexual immorality, or idolatry, yet Jesus rebukes them harshly and calls them dead.

## The Parasite of Blind Hypocrisy

The body of this church had been indwelt by a dangerous parasite, the parasite of blind hypocrisy. Blind meaning "unable to see;" hypocrisy meaning "the practice of professing beliefs, feelings, or virtues that one does not hold or possess; falseness."

This church was filled with nominal Christians: Christians who were unable to see that they were only professing to believe. They went through the motions: they went to church, they "played church," sang the songs, lifted their hands, called themselves Christians, and yet they were in reality spiritually dead. They were Christians in name only.

Today, in the twenty-first century Church many people call themselves Christians. In fact, church analyst George Barna comments that twenty million Americans call themselves Christians. They base this declaration on the fact that they are in good standing with a local church, many professing to serve somewhere in a local body. But we find the real truth in the fact that there are men, women, boys, and girls sitting in churches all over America—and the world— who have never had a transforming encounter with Jesus Christ. Or perhaps they did, but they have allowed life to lull them into a spiritual coma and now they have barely a heartbeat.

My heart was burdened for these people in Sardis, and all over the world who had, and have, fallen into blind hypocrisy. I asked the Lord to show me the characteristics of these unsaved churchgoers. The Lord led me to 2 Timothy 3:1-7:

> *[1]But mark this: There will be terrible times in the last days. [2]People will be lovers of themselves, lovers of money, boastful, proud, abusive, disobedient to their parents, ungrateful, unholy, [3]without love, unforgiving, slanderous, without self-control, brutal, not lovers of the good, [4]treacherous, rash, conceited, lovers of pleasure rather than lovers of God— [5]having a form of godliness but denying its power. Have nothing to do with them.*

> *[6]They are the kind who worm their way into homes and gain control over weak-willed women, who are loaded down with sins and are swayed by all kinds of evil desires, [7]always learning but never able to acknowledge the truth.*

Do you see what I see? These people will have a form of godliness but no power. What separates these people from true Christians is the Holy Spirit. What identifies them is by the absence of the Fruit of the Spirit. Let me insert a disclaimer here: we are all being raised from glory to glory and there is a process of sanctification. I'm not talking about perfection. I'm talking about fruit that becomes visible over time.

Is there evidence of love growing in your life? Is there evidence of self-control growing? Is there evidence of passion growing? Is there evidence of letting go of the things of the world and grabbing hold of the things of God? Does it grieve you to go against the Word of the Lord or do you justify your actions? Ask yourself, or more importantly, ask God to reveal the answers to you. Don't assume this is about your neighbor. God's Word is talking to you; *"He who has an ear, let him hear what the Spirit says to the churches."* Only God knows the true condition of your heart; He alone sees your vitals.

Several years ago my father was hospitalized for a collapsed lung. It was serious. Several doctors, specialists and surgeons were on call caring for my father. After several days in the hospital and multiple procedures, his condition seemed to get worse. One morning, while driving back to the hospital, I asked the Lord to tell me if my father was going to die. "Yes," was the immediate response I heard in my spirit.

Picking up the pace, I drove quickly to the hospital and upon arriving I became a bit of a drill sergeant. I ordered the doctors to begin life saving actions. I demanded other specialists be called in. Yet, in spite if my directives, no one moved any faster. In fact, at one point, one of the doctors boldly told me to stop freaking out. He said, "Tina, your father's vitals look good; he's going to be fine." This doctor even went so far as to walk me to the nurse's station so he could point out the readings on all of the monitoring machines.

But I knew the truth. I knew what the Lord had spoken to me. Within hours, my father's vitals began to show his true condition and with minutes of being transported to the ICU he was gone. I'll never forget the sound of the good doctor's voice, the one who told me to stop freaking out, as he spoke in no more than a whisper, "I'm so sorry, I just don't understand. His vitals looked good."

You may think your vitals look good, but only God knows for sure. However, I believe we can often recognize when something in our spiritual lives is out of whack, even if we can't put our finger on what it is. I beg of you as you read this chapter to ask the Lord Jesus Christ to search your heart and mind and reveal to you what He sees.

In verse 2, Jesus says to the Church of Sardis and to us today, *"Wake up!"*

*Wake up! Strengthen what remains and is about to die, for I have not found your deeds complete in the sight of my God.*

The use of these words "wake up" is written in the continuous—it literally means to wake up and stay awake. This would have been especially meaningful to the people of Sardis, given that both of their political defeats had come as a result of their watchmen sleeping on duty. Here Jesus was calling them to wake up, to take notice that something was missing in their faith walk; something was missing in their lives; even though everyone thought they were totally living right, Jesus is calling them to wake up!

What they were missing was an intimate relationship with the Lord evidenced by the Holy Spirit, alive and working in their hearts, granting them daily repentance, and helping them to live overcoming, victorious lives. We know from looking at Scripture, the Holy Spirit is the only one that can wake the dead and bring back the spiritually comatose.

It was in the Book of Ezekiel that the Holy Spirit moved and dry bones became living flesh. It's a spiritual law: only God's Spirit can move and truly wake us; but the Word of God can quicken us, stir us, shake us, disturb us, and convict us, creating an environment where not only our soul but our flesh is ready to surrender to the Holy Spirit.

In verse 2 Jesus says, *"Wake up! Strengthen what remains and is about to die . . . "* What was left? Only their physical bodies and their souls, which was made up of their emotions, minds, and personalities. Here we find Jesus saying if you don't wake up, you're not going to get the chance because He has not found your deeds complete in His sight. This church had been going through the motions, but without God. As a result, they are going to burn up as hay stubble with their works in their hands.

## Repent or Else!

Jesus has spoken to them strongly. He's told them the way it was; He now begins to give them direction. In verse 3 He says, *"Remember, therefore, what you have received and heard; obey it, and repent."*

What had they received and heard? My guess is like many of us, they had heard the gospel preached many, many times over. They may have even preached it themselves. Here Jesus is saying, "Do I have your attention enough for you test your own faith and ensure you are truly saved?" as Paul tells us to do in 2 Corinthians 13:5. Jesus says to remember what you have heard—the gospel, this time—obey it, and repent. He encourages them to truly repent, get on their faces and confess their sins, change their minds and their ways, and allow the Holy Spirit to begin to move in their lives.

He continues, *"But if you do not wake up, I will come like a thief and you will not know what time I will come to you."* Jesus promises us that judgment will be swift, sudden, and final should they not repent. This is a solid reminder that we may have our names in a roll book at church and still go to hell.

## God's Promises

In verse 4 Jesus says that in every church of blind hypocrites there are bound to be a few whose eyes have been opened. How good He is to acknowledge them in this letter. He tells them they will walk with Him, in this life and the next, wearing white because they are worthy. It is simply because they believe in Him and have been redeemed by His blood.

To those who overcome, Jesus gives a three-fold promise: they will walk with Him dressed in white; He will never blot out their names from the Book of Life; and He will acknowledge their names before God the Father and His angels.

The question of eternal security has haunted me since I became a believer. It's one of the major controversies between the denominations. Let's see what God says on the matter. Matthew 7:21-23 says,

> *"Not everyone who says to me, 'Lord, Lord,' will enter the kingdom of heaven, but only he who does the will of my Father who is in heaven. Many will say to me on that day, 'Lord, Lord, did we not prophesy in your name, and in your name drive out demons and perform many miracles?' Then I will tell them plainly, 'I never knew you. Away from me, you evildoers!'"*

This is a passage that has always disturbed me. On many occasions it's one the enemy has used to tempt me into believing I was not saved. One denomination taught you could say the sinner's prayer and be done with it. I now realize how incomplete that teaching is. Then another denomination I was a part of taught I needed to "keep up" salvation, work in faith for it. I now realize how incomplete that teaching is.

So I sought the Lord in my Spirit and in the Word of God. He was so good and so gracious to open my eyes to the truth and I feel that I absolutely must share with you what He showed me. My publishers have often instructed me to read my book backward to see new insights into my writing. Not surprisingly, the Lord suggested I use that same technique here.

First, do we understand that not everyone who does powerful things in Jesus' name is really filled with the Spirit of God? Okay, then how do these people do the powerful things? The answer is because the Holy Spirit may come on them, but not be in them. In Old Testament times, the Holy Spirit came "upon" men and women, but did not indwell them. We find in the Book of Acts that when the Holy Spirit came after the Ascension of Jesus, they were all filled with the Spirit (see Acts 2:4).

When the Holy Spirit comes on a person they can do anything that God permits because God can use both good and evil for His purposes. God's Spirit came upon Pharaoh, it came upon the Babylonians, and it came upon King Saul.

His Spirit brings power and an enabling. But remember we were instructed through Paul that if we have power, but have not love, we have nothing. Matthew 7:15-20 gives us another warning:

> *Watch out for false prophets. They come to you in sheep's clothing, but inwardly they are ferocious wolves. By their fruit you will recognize them. Do people pick grapes from thorn bushes, or figs from thistles?*

*Likewise every good tree bears good fruit, but a bad tree bears bad fruit. A good tree cannot bear bad fruit and a bad tree cannot bear good fruit. Every tree that does not bear good fruit is cut down and thrown into the fire. Thus, by their fruit you will recognize them.*

Jesus said, *"By their fruit you will recognize them"*— the fruit of love, joy, peace, patience, kindness, goodness, faithfulness, gentleness, and self-control. Supernatural fruit, supernatural increase.

Jesus cautions us again in Matthew 7:13-14:

*"Enter through the narrow gate. For wide is the gate and broad is the road that leads to destruction, and many enter through it. But small is the gate and narrow the road that leads to life, and only a few find it."*

Friends, we are saved by the grace of God for it is indeed a free gift, but it is a gift we must receive daily through an overcoming faith.

Taking it one step further, I want to suggest to you the Christian walk is like a series of gates. Each one gets smaller and narrower. It requires us to exhibit more faith and bear more fruit, to believe more deeply and exhibit supernatural fruit. It's not that we lose our salvation if we blow it. It's that we walk out our salvation by the fruit and power of the Spirit.

The Church of Sardis was told to strengthen what they had left. I believe this church had God's anointing power, but did not have His fullness as evidenced by His fruit. Is there any possibility He is saying the same to you today? Are you sure you have both?

# FOOD FOR THOUGHT

| FRUIT OF THE SPIRIT | ROTTEN FRUIT OF THE WORLD |
| --- | --- |
| Love | Lovers of themselves; money; pleasure |
| Goodness | Boastful, proud, conceited |
| Patience | Abusiveness |
| Goodness | Disobedience to parents |
| Joy | Ungrateful |
| Faithfulness | Unholy |
| Gentleness | Slanderous, treacherous |
| Self control | Without self control, rash |
| Gentleness | Brutality |
| Peace | Not lovers of the good or God |

# 12

# Philadelphia

Now we come to the sixth letter to the sixth angel of the sixth church, the Church of Philadelphia, found in Revelation 3:7-13:

*⁷To the angel of the church in Philadelphia write:*

*These are the words of him who is holy and true, who holds the key of David. What he opens no one can shut, and what he shuts no one can open. ⁸I know your deeds. See, I have placed before you an open door that no one can shut. I know that you have little strength, yet you have kept my word and have not denied my name.*

*⁹I will make those who are of the synagogue of Satan, who claim to be Jews though they are not, but are liars—I will make them come and fall down at your feet and acknowledge that I have loved you. ¹⁰Since you have kept my command to endure patiently, I will also keep you from the hour of trial that is going to come upon the whole world to test those who live on the earth.*

*[11]I am coming soon. Hold on to what you have, so that no one will take your crown. [12]Him who overcomes I will make a pillar in the temple of my God. Never again will he leave it. I will write on him the name of my God and the name of the city of my God, the new Jerusalem, which is coming down out of heaven from my God; and I will also write on him my new name. [13]He who has an ear, let him hear what the Spirit says to the churches.*

Philadelphia was located twenty-eight miles southeast of Sardis as we continue on our road trip through Asia Minor, known to us today as modern day Turkey. Philadelphia was uniquely located as a border town and was positioned on a trade route. It was often referred to as "the gateway to the east" because the Greeks used it to take their language and culture to neighboring cities.

Interestingly, Philadelphia was named after a king in Pergamum who was nicknamed Philadelphus, and who was very fond of and loyal to his brother. (Which is why today Philadelphia, Pennsylvania is called "The City of Brotherly Love.") In honor of this king, the citizens of Pergamum traveled to an uncharted territory and founded this city, Philadelphia, in his honor.

There were three unique things about this city: it had volcanic soil which made it ideal for growing grapes and making wine; there were many hot springs in the area where people would come in hope of receiving health and healing; and the city was built on a geographic fault line which made it prone to earthquakes.

Several earthquakes had devastated the city and it had been rebuilt several times. It was very frustrating for those who lived there because for years after an earthquake, the aftershocks would shake the city's very foundations. As a result it was common for the citizens of Philadelphia to come and go, moving in and out of the city. Out when the aftershocks occurred, in when they were over. People were continually passing through the "door" of Philadelphia. This will prove important as we study this letter.

## The Church of Philadelphia

Within this city we find the Church of Philadelphia. It was a little known church, given this letter is the only place we find any mention of it. Everything we learn about the church will be discovered right here in these six verses. The most important observation to be made is, once again, Jesus breaks from His Oreo cookie method of feedback. The Church of Philadelphia receives no rebuke of any kind. The Church of Smyrna, the persecuted church, was the only other church of these seven with such a distinction.

Just because this church does not receive a rebuke doesn't mean it's a perfect church; there's no such thing. It simply means in the eyes of Jesus—the eyes that are holy and true (verse 7)—He is choosing to simply affirm and encourage. I would take this to mean this is a church Jesus smiles upon and is pleased with, and it is a church from which we can learn much.

It is also interesting to note that how Jesus introduces himself to each church is always vital to what He is about to say to them. He says in verse 7:

> "These are the words of him who is holy and true, who holds the key to David. What he opens no one can shut, and what he shuts no one can open."

Jesus begins by reminding us that He is holy and true. And, obviously, you can't have one without the other. He continues by saying He holds the key of David. What does a key do for you? It allows access into someplace or something. It gives you rights and authority. If I have a key to a building, I have the authority to be there any time I desire.

At first glance we might be tempted to think this key is the same key referred to in Revelation 1:18, when Jesus told the Apostle John not to be afraid because He is the first and the last and that He is alive and holds the keys to death and Hades. But that's not what he's referring to here.

Jesus is telling the Church of Philadelphia He is the one with sovereign authority, who makes the decisions about who comes and goes in His Church and in His Kingdom. He is the one who decides who can serve God and who can't, and who He will bless and who He won't. That is very important to the church in Philadelphia as we will see, but the Old Testament is where this teaching comes from.

## A bit of history: Isaiah 22

Isaiah 22:15-24 will give us background before continuing in Revelation 3.

> *<sup></sup>*<sup></sup>¹⁵ *This is what the Lord, the LORD Almighty, says: "Go, say to this steward, to Shebna, who is in charge of the palace:* ¹⁶ *What are you doing here and who gave you permission to cut out a grave for yourself here, hewing your grave on the height and chiseling your resting place in the rock?*

> ¹⁷ *"Beware, the LORD is about to take firm hold of you and hurl you away, O you mighty man.* ¹⁸ *He will roll you up tightly like a ball and throw you into a large country. There you will die and there your splendid chariots will remain—you disgrace to your master's house!*

*¹⁹ I will depose you from your office, and you will be
ousted from your position.*

*²⁰ "In that day I will summon my servant, Eliakim
son of Hilkiah. ²¹ I will clothe him with your robe and
fasten your sash around him and hand your authority
over to him. He will be a father to those who live in
Jerusalem and to the house of Judah. ²² I will place on
his shoulder the key to the house of David; what he
opens no one can shut, and what he shuts no one can
open. ²³I will drive him like a peg into a firm place; he
will be a seat of honor for the house of his father. ²⁴ All
the glory of his family will hang on him: its offspring
and offshoots—all its lesser vessels, from the bowls to
all the jars."*

For the sake of context, in verses 15-19, the prophet Isaiah
gives a message from God that Shebna, a high court official,
was about to be replaced as a steward in King Hezekiah's
palace. A steward was a manager of the royal household—
equivalent to a prime minister or a secretary of state. He had
a very responsible position, but Shebna became corrupt and
had begun using his power for personal gain. As a result,
God removed him from his position. This passage refers to
his replacement, Eliakim, and we see reference to the key of
David that will enlarge our understanding as to what it means
and how it relates to the Church of Philadelphia.

Eliakim, a faithful servant of God, is appointed as a
steward, a manager over the king's household, to replace
the Shebna who was unfaithful. Upon his promotion, King
Hezekiah, under the authority of God, gives Eliakim a key to
the door of the palace, a key to the house of David. This key
to the "the house of David" is a sign for all to see that he had
authority over the house of David. This means that Eliakim,
above all others, had the authority to determine who could be

admitted into the palace and the king's presence, and who was to be kept out. Additionally, it meant he could decide who to bless out of the king's treasury and who not to bless. It also meant he could determine who could serve the king as a part of the king's household.

Relating this back to the passage in Revelation 3, we see Jesus saying to the Church of Philadelphia that He holds the key of David, and He has the ability to open and shut doors. This is especially meaningful. Jesus tells them in Revelation 3:8 He knows they've been faithful to His Word and His name, and as a result He promises to make those who are of the synagogue of Satan worship at their feet and acknowledge that they are loved by Him.

What does this have to do with the key of David? It has everything to do with it and it's where we find a lurking parasite. Commentators believe in this passage Jesus gives us a clue that there was more than one church operating in the city of Philadelphia: a church with people who claim to be Jews but Jesus calls liars; a group of people much like those in Sardis who were blind hypocrites; a group of people who were perhaps Jews by blood, but not by faith; a group of Jews who had kicked the Jewish and Gentile Christians out because they weren't "good or clean enough."

Jesus says to the Church of Philadelphia, *"I know your deeds;"* In essence, He's saying, "I know that you had to leave and start another church because a door had been slammed in your face." Here He says to them not to worry about that door because He is the God who is holy and true, He has sovereign authority on all the doors that really matter.

## The Parasite of Iadequacy

And here, right here, we get our first glimpse at the parasite that has made its way into the Church of Philadelphia. In verse 8 Jesus says, *"I know that you have little strength . . ."* This word *strength* is the same one we get the word dynamite from. It's a word that means miracle-working power.

As I thought about this church, I wondered why they had so little power. After all, they had their own church; they could minister as they saw fit internally and externally; and then I understood. This church did have a parasite. Remember a parasite draws its power from the host, so the fact this church had little strength told me something was robbing it of its power.

What was it? What was the parasite? May I suggest that the Church of Philadelphia had the parasites of inferiority and inadequacy? Inferiority meaning lower in rank, standing, degree, quality or value. Inadequacy meaning failing to reach an expected or required level or standard.

How do I know? Because I have been intimately acquainted with this one. I remember the knowing glances I received because I was a worldly outsider. I have been around missionaries, preachers, and people who wouldn't give me the time of day because I was not born and bred under the correct denominational banner or with the right pedigree. Maybe you have experienced this, too. I know what it's like to be humored when God gives me a word, or not respected to teach and preach because I don't have the proper credentials.

You see, the enemy knows if he can plant a seed in your mind that says, "I don't fit in, I'm not good enough," or "They are better," then he's won the battle. He knows if he can take that seed and nurture it in us through his accusations and evil affirmations, we will do one of two things.

We will shrink back, wither, and die . . . or we will become hard and brittle.

Either way, he's won. That's why I believe in verse 11, Jesus tells the Church of Philadelphia to hold on to what they have so that no one could take their crown. This word *crown* is not the crown of life, but a crown of honor. The Church of Philadelphia was a body honored by Jesus himself. It didn't matter what anyone else thought of them. He wanted them to know "you are honored by me." Based upon His promises in verses 12-13, Jesus wanted everyone else to know as well.

## The Promises of God

In verse 12 Jesus says, *"Him who overcomes I will make a pillar in the temple of my God."* This promise would have been very special to the Church of Philadelphia because history records that during each earthquake that devastated the city, the only thing ever left standing were the pillars—big, tall, concrete pillars. Jesus' promise to the Church of Philadelphia that if they will stand strong—not with a little strength, but stand strong in His power—when all the others have fallen away, they will become pillars on which God's glory will rest.

History also tells us when people returned after an earthquake or aftershock, they would write their names on one of these pillars to show they had made it home safely. They would communicate by signing their names to the pillar, letting everyone know they had overcome the circumstances. It might say something like "the Blounts are here" or "the Millers are here." Jesus knows this about them, so in verse 12 He speaks to them in a language they will understand.

He also promises them if they will overcome, not only will God make them pillars, but that He will do the writing this time. He will write God's name all over them. He will write it in such a way that everyone will know they are living for the New Jerusalem, where we will live for all eternity. It's a promise for the future but it's also a promise for the here and now. A promise to be truly set apart as those who have been shaken and stirred, yet are still withstanding.

Lastly, Jesus promises them if they will just hold on, be strong, and overcome the parasites of inadequacy and inferiority, He will write His name on them also. Tattoo it for all to see. They will be, in essence, "walking pillars of God's glory."

## Making It Real

I want you to remember He is talking to us—to you and to me. I believe Jesus wants us to know that we don't have worry about what others think of us. We don't have to feel inadequate; we can choose to reject that parasite. You see, the Apostle Paul tells us in 2 Corinthians 12:9 that God's grace is sufficient for you, because His power is made perfect in our weakness.

My heart's prayer is that if you related in any way to this beautiful Body of Christ in Philadelphia, like Paul you will learn to boast all the more gladly about your weaknesses, so that Christ's power may rest on you.

# 13

# Laodicea

We come to the seventh letter to the seventh angel of the seventh church, the Church of Laodicea. This church is revealed to us in Revelation 3:14-22:

*¹⁴To the angel of the church in Laodicea write:*

*These are the words of the Amen, the faithful and true witness, the ruler of God's creation. ¹⁵I know your deeds, that you are neither cold nor hot. I wish you were either one or the other! ¹⁶So, because you are lukewarm—neither hot nor cold—I am about to spit you out of my mouth.*

*¹⁷You say, 'I am rich; I have acquired wealth and do not need a thing.' But you do not realize that you are wretched, pitiful, poor, blind and naked. ¹⁸I counsel you to buy from me gold refined in the fire, so you can become rich; and white clothes to wear, so you can cover your shameful nakedness; and salve to put on your eyes, so you can see.*

*[19]Those whom I love I rebuke and discipline. So be earnest, and repent. [20]Here I am! I stand at the door and knock. If anyone hears my voice and opens the door, I will come in and eat with him, and he with me. [21]To him who overcomes, I will give the right to sit with me on my throne, just as I overcame and sat down with my Father on his throne.*

*[22]He who has an ear, let him hear what the Spirit says to the churches."*

We have come to the last of the letters Jesus inspired the Apostle John to write and, to put it mildly, this church was in the worst spiritual condition of any we have seen so far. But before we go any further, we should find out about the city itself. Laodicea was under the rule of the Roman government just like all the other cities in the region. It was a wealthy city; in fact, it was the wealthiest city in the province.

While many trades were housed in this city, it's important to note that three main industries contributed most of Laodicea's wealth. First, Laodicea was the banking hub of the area. Second, it was known for its textile industry, which manufactured a very rare, glossy black wool. Third, it housed a medical school that produced, among other things, a specialized eye salve.

Laodicea was located forty miles southeast of Philadelphia and was sandwiched, within thirty miles, in between the cities of Hierapolis and Colossae. Colossae was the city to which Paul wrote his letter to the Colossians. In fact, if you read the Book of Colossians you'll see that while Paul never visited Laodicea, he had a very special place in his heart for the believers there and wanted to ensure his letter to the Colossians made it to them as well.

Their location in relation to these other cities was very important because Laodicea had a problem: a water problem, to be exact. The problem was they didn't have any usable water—but their neighbors did. The city of Hierapolis was known for their hot springs. Much like the city of Philadelphia, people would travel to these hot springs because of their medicinal attributes. Colossae, on the other hand, was known for its icy cold mountain water. Laodicea didn't have either. It was located along the Lycus River—basically a pool of unusable, tainted water.

Because of this, the Roman government built an underground aqueduct that piped in water from their neighboring cities. Some might have thought, "Problem solved." But the problem wasn't solved. Because by the time the water arrived in the city of Laodicea, it wasn't hot anymore, nor was it cold anymore. It was lukewarm, tepid, and often tainted.

History records that visitors to the region who were unaware of the water issues would dip into a well after a long journey hoping to find a refreshing drink, and would spew the water out of their mouths because it was so foul. These facts about the city and its water will prove very important as we study this church.

## The Church of Laodicea

As with many of the churches we've studied so far, the Church of Laodicea mirrored the city of Laodicea. It was very, very wealthy. So wealthy that after it had been demolished by an earthquake years earlier, it rejected the help of the Roman government because there was enough money to rebuild it without anyone's financial support. They didn't ask for money from the bank or the state or the government; they paid for it out of their own pockets.

History records it to be a beautiful church, not lacking in any respect. That tells us that if the church had enough money to take care of itself, then the body of believers that made up the church had more than enough money to meet all their own personal needs and desires. That fact comes into play as Jesus begins to introduce himself in His salutation.

*14 " To the angel of the church in Laodicea write: These are the words of the Amen, the faithful and true witness, the ruler of God's creation."*

Jesus introduces himself as the Amen, the faithful and true witness, the ruler of God's creation. The way Jesus describes himself as is as important as what He says. Let's break this verse down just a bit to get a clear picture in our minds of who He is.

He begins, *"These are the words of the Amen."* What do you think that means? Think of when a preacher is preaching and you respond to something he says with "Amen." What do you mean? That you agree, yes? That's what the word *Amen* means here: "Trustworthy," as in "So be it." Couple that with what He says next—that He is " . . . *the faithful and true witness."* He puts a bow on top by reminding them He is " . . . *the ruler of God's creation."* Tie all that together and we see that He is saying, "I am a trustworthy, faithful, and true witness."

Whenever He speaks we should receive His words and be able to take them to the bank. We should also respond by saying, "So be it," because He is the first and the last, the beginning and the end. Why did He use such a distinctive introduction? I'd like to suggest it's because He knows that what He's about to say is going to land hard on some hearts. There are going to be some who don't want to receive His words as true, and might be tempted to argue with Him just a bit. Jesus knew there were men and women in the church who were not going to agree with His perception of their spiritual state, so right from the start the He sets the stage.

I believe knowing what is going to happen, Jesus opens the letter to the Church of Laodicea by saying, "I am the Amen." To put another way, "It doesn't matter how you see things, I AM the Lord and I get the first and the *last* word."

We need to remember that what was true of Laodicea is true of all of us. No one wants to be rebuked by the Lord, but we must remember that when the Lord rebukes us it's out of His great love for us (see Proverbs 13:18). It's so important not to harden our hearts when the Word of the Lord comes. We must allow Him to speak to us, minister to us, rebuke us, and convict us. I've been on the receiving end of God's rebuke and, I'm sad to say, I've learned a few ways to stonewall Him whenever He's trying to get my attention. I wonder if you do as well?

Some of us simply turn up the noise of life and drown Him out. Others get real busy. Still others try to justify their actions to God. Still more of us simply harden our hearts and assume He couldn't be talking to us. I want to remind you in the words of the inspired author of Hebrews 3:7-8, *"Today, if you hear his voice, do not harden your hearts."* As you read through the letter to the Church of Laodicea, I invite you to allow the Word of the Lord to become intimate, and resist any urge to stonewall Him. Remember that those He loves, He corrects.

## No Affirmation or Commendation

In verse 15 of our text, we see that after introducing himself to the Church of Laodicea, Jesus gets right to the double stuff rebuke. This church receives no affirmation and no commendation of any kind. Jesus doesn't affirm even one person within this congregation.

Read verses 15-16:

*I know your deeds, that you are neither cold nor hot. I wish you were either one or the other! So, because you are lukewarm—neither hot nor cold—I am about to spit you out of my mouth.*

He begins by saying, *"I know your deeds."* He is saying, I know you. In other words, don't try to argue with what I'm about to say, "I know you."

Jesus already told them that. He said it in His introduction: He knows it all, so when He says, *"I know your deeds,"* it is said in such as way as to stop all possible evasion of the truth. It's to make them sit up and take notice. In verse 15, Jesus continues, *"You are neither cold nor hot. I wish you were either one or the other! So because you are . . . neither hot nor cold—I am about to spit you out of my mouth."*

What is He referencing here? He's alluding to their spiritual state, but he's using their physical state to do it. He'll do the same with you and me. He'll address something we can immediately relate to and get our attention in another area.

Not long ago God spoke to me through a devotional and told me to get my house in order. That happened to be a day I had already planned to clean my house. It wasn't until later I realized that He was talking about an entirely different matter. He's doing the same thing here. He's referring to the state of the water in their city and relating it to the state of the living water within them.

As I pondered this, I began to wonder about the *way* Jesus said what He said. Why didn't He just say, "I wish you were hot?" Why did He say He wished they were either one or the other? Why hot or cold?

To answer that question we have to identify what it means to be hot or cold, as well as recognizing what it means to be lukewarm. I want to suggest to you that in overly simplistic terms there are three kinds of spiritual conditions:

1. Hot as it's used in this context means fervent or extremely passionate. We see this described several times in Scripture. For example, in Acts 18:24-26 (KJV), it says:

   *And a certain Jew named Apollos, born at Alexandria, an eloquent man, and mighty in the scriptures, came to Ephesus. ²⁵This man was instructed in the way of the Lord; and being fervent in the spirit, he spake and taught diligently the things of the Lord, knowing only the baptism of John.*

   *²⁶And he began to speak boldly in the synagogue: whom when Aquila and Priscilla had heard, they took him unto them, and expounded unto him the way of God more perfectly.*

   Here we see a man so passionate you can't hush him up even though his knowledge is limited.

2. Cold, on the other hand, used in this context means the exact opposite. It means to have no passion at all toward God or the things of God. Commentators agree that two types of individuals fit into this category: those who have never heard the Word of God before and those who outright reject it. These aren't pretenders. Rather they are individuals who, by choice, serve another god or through ignorance don't know about Jesus because they've never heard the gospel.

3. Lukewarm—what does it mean to be lukewarm? It means neither fervently passionate nor ice cold. It

means you can take God or leave Him. Perhaps it means taking God when it fits into your schedule, but casting Him aside when something more interesting beckons. It also means you were one or the other at one point in time. I know that because no one is born lukewarm. To become lukewarm there must be either a cooling off period or a slow warming that stopped somewhere along the way.

Let me ask you . . . based on these definitions of hot, cold and lukewarm, why would Jesus say, "I wish you were either hot or cold"? I can comprehend why He'd want us to be hot. But why would cold be so much more desirable than lukewarm?

Let me suggest it's because it is easier to reach the heart of a person who is hot or cold rather than lukewarm. You see, people who think they are righteous are the hardest hearts to reach. Those who think they are just fine spiritually don't respond to the convicting arrows of the Holy Spirit.

This happens in many different ways. Some fall into the routine of "doing church," without ever truly applying the Word of God to their own hearts and lives. For others it happens while serving, but forgetting who they're serving and why. For still others it happens during a season of loss; when God doesn't come through the way they thought He should. As a result, a guard goes up around their hearts and they say, "I'll go through the motions, but I won't love you anymore." It can happen in so many ways if we are not careful. Let's find out how it happened for the Church of Laodicea.

Laodicea had rebuilt their church after being devastated from an earthquake in AD 62. We know they accepted no help from any one, including the Roman government. Commentators agree this was the turning point for their church. It was during this time they became self-sufficient, and they perceived they needed help from no one. It was that self-sufficiency that opened the door to a parasite: the parasite of complacency.

## The Parasite of Complacency

Complacency by definition means to be self-satisfied and unaware of danger. When the Laodecians became self-satisfied they accidentally and slowly put out the fire in their own lives. When they no longer needed God or looked to Him for His guidance and support, they opened the back door to this dangerous parasite.

I am currently coaching a former executive of a Fortune 500 company. He retired a few years back, but due to the economy draining away all of his retirement he's found himself in the job market again. Recently, we were discussing where he wanted to go next in his career and he began to share his heart with me.

He told me of being very poor as a little boy and working his way up, far beyond his upbringing, to a place of worldly success and material wealth. I asked him specifically to what he attributed his success in life. He responded, "Hard work and luck." A little later in the conversation he revealed a bit more of his heart by saying, "Tina, I'm in a situation that I can't seem to find a way out of." He continued, "It's the first time this has ever happened in my life. I've always been able to find a way out." In that moment, the Holy Spirit nudged me and I prayed that God would give me an opportunity to speak into his life.

As we prepared to close our call, I asked him for permission to share something I had observed and he agreed. I reminded him that in one of our earlier calls he told me he was a man of faith, a praying man, a former Sunday school teacher who attended church regularly. Yet I observed the fact that when he shared with me what had contributed to his success, there was no mention of God at all.

I suggested there was a very real possibility he was placed in a life situation that was difficult enough to turn his whole heart back to God, not just part of it. As if by confirmation, a few days later he sent me a reference written by a former colleague who ended with these words: *Jack is a self-made man.* Through this observation, the Lord confirmed that wealth and success had slowly eaten away at Jack's passionate fervor for God and the things of God. Sadly, Jack has yet to acknowledge either the parasite of spiritual complacency or the root of his self-sufficiency. As a result, at this writing, he remains lukewarm and continues to slowly lose not only his possessions, but also his passion for life.

That's exactly what happened to the Church of Laodicea as we see in verse 17. Jesus says to them, *"You say, 'I am rich; I have acquired wealth and do not need a thing.' But you do not realize that you are wretched, pitiful, poor, blind and naked."* This church had allowed its financial abundance to woo itself into a state of complacency. This is just one example of how Christians can become lukewarm. There are many others.

What are the possibilities? Perhaps some Christians have accepted Christ as Savior but never as Lord, and as a result they have one foot at the Cross and the other foot in the world. Perhaps they once had a passionate relationship with Jesus Christ, but over time they have allowed their relationship to cool. Maybe they have been living off an inherited faith for years instead of pursuing their own relationship with God. Perhaps they've been living so long in "churchianity"—going through all the rituals—that they've lost sight of Christianity. There's also the very real possibility God just hasn't performed, supplied, or cared for them in the way they desired, and as a result they've taken up an offense—an offense toward God, toward the church, or other Christians. These are just a few of the ways it can happen.

For the Laodiceans it was money, but we each have a responsibility to think how it might happen, or has happened, in our own lives because there are serious consequences to staying lukewarm. The Lord tells us in verse 16 how He feels about lukewarm Christians.

He views their faith or rather lack of as disgusting and distasteful, so repulsive He was about to spit them out of His mouth. This word *spit* here means to violently vomit. It's a real word picture and Jesus said it intentionally. The Lord had very strong feelings about the self-sufficiency of Laodicea and He has the very same reaction in dealing with you and me.

As we have learned, when the earthquake devastated Laodicea, including the church, this body was so self-reliant they rejected the help of the Roman government. This is in contrast to other churches we've studied, such as Philadelphia. Tacitus, a Roman historian, is quoted as saying of that era, "Laodicea arose from the ruins by the strength of her own resources and with no help from us."

Laodicea is no different from many of us in the world today. I'm thinking of a famous athlete at the moment who was idolized for his performance and his money until scandal revealed he wasn't who he proclaimed to be. We are reminded in 1 Samuel 16:7 that the Lord does not look at the things man looks at. Man looks at the outward appearance, but the Lord looks at the heart

In verse 17 we see Jesus doesn't say you are "healthy, wealthy, and wise;" He tells them, " . . . *you are wretched, pitiful, poor, blind and naked.*" Can you just imagine the shock they felt? I can because God has said it to me. During a time when I was trying to handle a situation all on my own, God spoke these exact words to me. I remember feeling as though the Lord had just struck me, and in truth that's exactly what He did. He gave me a spiritual spanking and you know what? I deserved it. Is there any possibility He is quickening your heart as well? If so, I so encourage you to fall on your face before Him. I can tell you from personal experience, it's the only appropriate response.

I can just imagine the Church of Laodicea in their fine clothing and jewelry, sitting on their fat wallets, and thinking, "Uh, Jesus, I think You sent us the wrong letter." Yet, that is exactly why He used the water example; it quickened something in their spirits. He does the same with you and me. When Jesus talks to us He will usually speak to us in such a way that we know what He wants us to do. He sees through all the masks we put on and gets quickly to the heart of the matter.

You see, when Jesus saw the Church of Laodicea, He didn't see them in their earthly splendor. He saw them sitting in filthy rags, tainted with sin. Yet, make no mistake, although He saw them in their state of sin, it was His love for them that brought about the rebuke. He loved them so much He longed for this church to open their eyes and see clearly.

Money is one of those areas that has the ability to skew the vision, but it's not the only one. The Church of Laodicea had lots of money, but it was poor. Contrast this to the Church of Smyrna, which was financially poor, yet Jesus called them rich. Both were blind to their true spiritual condition until Jesus spoke to them.

So where was the disconnect? How could one church be so blind while the other church was so enlightened? Moreover, how do we ensure that we are not also wretched, pitiful, poor, blind, and naked? I want to suggest it's a matter of focus.

In Matthew 6:22-23, the apostle gives us some light on the subject when he says:

> *22"The eye is the lamp of the body. If your eyes are good, your whole body will be full of light.²³But if your eyes are bad, your whole body will be full of darkness. If then the light within you is darkness, how great is that darkness!*

Now, let's look at it again in The King James Version:

> *²²The light of the body is the eye: if therefore thine eye be single, thy whole body shall be full of light. ²³But if thine eye be evil, thy whole body shall be full of darkness. If therefore the light that is in thee be darkness, how great is that darkness!*

What is the key line in these verses? It is simply "If thine eye be single." This passage means having one heartfelt purpose, focusing on a single object. In this case, in our case, it's Christ alone. In verse 23, we see that having an evil eye actually means having a diseased, split eye; one that has a dual focus. Perhaps this is a result of the parasite of complacency and self-sufficiency.

Now apply this to our Church of Laodicea. It wasn't that this church didn't have a heart for God; it was that their vision was not singularly focused. That's what having a blind heart means. It doesn't mean not being able to see at all. It means having smoky vision. This church could see, they just couldn't see clearly. The object of their affection—worldly possessions—had skewed their vision and had stolen their fire and their passion. As a result they had cooled and become lukewarm.

In spite of their straying hearts, notice the gentle way Jesus speaks to them. Remember He just gave them the lion's roar and now He loves them as though they were lost lambs. He says, *"I counsel you,"* meaning, I am the wonderful counselor and I'm giving you some fatherly advice here, *". . . buy from me gold refined in the fire."*

Gold they had plenty of, but this was the refiner's gold. The Apostle Paul tells us in Colossians 2 that it is the hidden treasures of wisdom and knowledge found only in Christ. This kind of gold is only purchased by tossing into the fire all of the other things that keep us in a state of self-sufficiency. Jesus is calling them—and us—to trust in Him alone. In John 15, Jesus reminds us that the Father cuts off every branch that bears no fruit. Might I suggest that you allow Him to purge your tree and use the pruned limbs as firewood to heat up your passion for Him?

In verse 18 we see that Jesus says if they will trust in Him alone, they will become truly rich, truly well dressed, and will have the ability to see clearly. Remember the three main industries in Laodicea were banking, textile, and an eye clinic. In other words, He's saying, "I'll trade you." You give up your heart for money and I'll give you true riches. You stop focusing on your shiny black wool and I'll dress you in white. You stop trying to put ointment on your eyes and I'll help you really see.

Jesus loved this church in spite of their parasite. He loves you in spite of yours. He doesn't want to spit us out of His mouth. Jesus tells them, *"I stand at the door and knock,"* if any of you will answer the call I will come in and save you, cleanse you, and dine with you. Yet the underlying message remains the same: if we do not heed His call, if we continue to stay in a state of complacency and self-sufficiency, on the Day of Judgment, He will spit us out of His mouth.

He, who has ear, let him hear what the spirit says to the churches.

# 14

# Protecting

## THE BACK DOOR

Like rain from Heaven, God dropped this study into my heart and it has taken on a life of its own for me. It's a message I believe God is so passionate about because He desires that no one should perish, no not one. You know my story; it was birthed out of a medical situation I experienced when a doctor unknowingly implanted a parasite into my body—a body parasite so evil that, had it lived, would have caused me to go blind.

It was a situation I was fearful over and, truthfully, felt a great deal of shame about. Even though it wasn't my fault, there was just something gross about thinking there was a worm living on the inside of me. I remember sitting in the infectious disease doctor's office and wanting nothing more than to be made invisible every time another patient walked in. I remember not wanting to meet the nurse's eyes as she asked me about my diagnosis.

I had a parasite; a parasite I believe was placed inside me by the hands of the enemy. Through careful observance of my life, he waited until my circumstances allowed him an opening into my physical body. Now some would argue that it was just bad luck, but I disagree. I believe the enemy meant it for my harm. But I now know that what the enemy meant for evil, God turned around for my good; and, it is my hope, for your good as well.

As I pondered how I would close this book, I asked the Lord for inspiration. I asked Him for direction and guidance. I asked Him for a nugget we could deposit into the bank of our lives that would teach us a godly principle; one that would allow us to guard our lives against the enemy of our souls so we don't become like many of the churches we've studied. I wanted to know how we could protect the Body of Christ so a parasite could not make its way in. I was amazed at how quickly the words came from Him. They were not audible, but in my spirit I heard the Lord say, "Teach them to put on the armor of God."

With that direction from the Lord, we'll go to Ephesians 6:10-18 for our closing thoughts:

> [10]*Finally, be strong in the Lord and in his mighty power.* [11]*Put on the full armor of God so that you can take your stand against the devil's schemes.* [12]*For our struggle is not against flesh and blood, but against the rulers, against the authorities, against the powers of this dark world and against the spiritual forces of evil in the heavenly realms.*
>
> [13]*Therefore put on the full armor of God, so that when the day of evil comes, you may be able to stand your ground, and after you have done everything, to stand.* [14]*Stand firm then, with the belt of truth buckled around your waist, with the breastplate of righteousness in place,* [15]*and with your feet fitted with the readiness that comes from the gospel of peace.* [16]*In addition to all this, take up the shield of faith, with which you can*

*extinguish all the flaming arrows of the evil one. [17]Take the helmet of salvation and the sword of the Spirit, which is the word of God.*

*[18]And pray in the Spirit on all occasions with all kinds of prayers and requests. With this in mind, be alert and always keep on praying for all the saints.*

The Apostle Paul ended his letter to the Church of Ephesus with this strong instruction. Yet, as many of the letters Paul wrote, it's believed to have been written not only for one church, but also for all of the churches in the area of Asia Minor. This letter was written to encourage each church; to help every church we have studied become the overcomers Christ had called them to be. As we know from Jesus' letters, some listened, some didn't. Today, we have the same opportunity to listen and heed instructions that will protect us from deadly enemy-sent parasites.

Starting with verse 10, we are told to be strong in the Lord and in his mighty power. Would it be fair to say that life can be hard? Downright tough? Would you agree with me that it can kick the living stew out of you? Truthfully, I'm not sure how unbelievers cope. I know their coping mechanisms because I used to have many of them myself. Yet now that I know the truth, the thought of going through life alone without God is more than my mind can comprehend.

This verse reminds us that this thing called life can only be lived victoriously if we are doing it in God's power. That's the meaning of this verse; it literally means to be enabled by God's power. If you have been saved, but have not been baptized in the Holy Spirit, you are missing a key ingredient to victorious living. Allow me to encourage you to seek it today. It will radically change your life!

In verses 11-13, Paul is telling us to put on the full armor of God: not part of it, all of it. It's important to God that we put on His full armor; so important that He tells us twice, once in verse 11 and again in verse 13.

I have learned there are three components of the armor, which are:

- **Integuments**: a word that means a natural covering, similar to skin

  - Breastplate

  - Belt/girdle

  - Shoes

- **Defensive armor:** designed for protection

  - Helmet

  - Shield

- **Offensive weapons:** used when attacking an enemy

  - Sword (God's Word/Bible)

  - Spear (Prayer)

Individually these are all good components, but it's in unity and consistency we'll find the power to stand. *Stand*—it's a word that we find four times in these passages. Now I don't know about you, but I think of the word *stand* as a passive word. I stand at the grocery store. I stand in line at the bank. I even stand to sing a hymn at church. You get the picture. But that's not what this word means. To stand actually means "to abide," which means to live out, await, and withstand.

Let's put it all together: this passage of Scripture is telling us that (1) we need to be filled with the Holy Spirit so (2) we have the power to live out the Christian life to (3) await Jesus' return and (4) withstand the attacks of the enemy while we live on planet Earth.

As I think about the seven churches we've studied, we find each church was attacked by a parasite directly in their minds. That parasite may have affected their hearts, mouths, feet, hands, and even their loins, but the seed always began in their minds. Remember that as we begin to look at the part of the armor that should be like a second skin to us, a spiritual skin.

Verse 14 tells us to stand firm with the belt of truth buckled around our waists. The KJV says to gird your waist. That was common language in Bible days and it meant to get ready for battle, because warriors put on their girdle belt when they were going off to war. To gird yourselves, or put on the belt of truth, simply means to know what you're fighting for and why. Do you know why you make faith choices every day? What's your truth? Why Jesus?

I also want you to see that girdles or belts in those days not only went around the waist, but they also protected the loin area of the warrior's body. One commentator wrote that the loin has reproductive, procreative power. So, we protect the part of our body that creates or produces truth. In other words, what we believe will become our truth and what becomes our truth will be reproduced in our lives and the lives of others by our choices, actions, and reactions. Our truth begins by reading the words in red. In John 8:31-32, Jesus said, *"If you hold to my teaching, you are really my disciples. Then you will know the truth and the truth will set you free."* Jesus' teaching needs to become like second skin to us.

Then we're told have the breastplate of righteousness in place. Here Paul is talking about our character, the Fruit of the Spirit being lived out in our lives every day—love, joy, peace, patience, kindness, goodness, faithfulness, gentleness, and self-control. He says to have these in place all the time. They come from abiding in Jesus (see John 15).

The third integument comes in the form of having our feet fitted with the readiness that comes from the gospel of peace. Our feet are the part of our bodies that hold us up and move us forward. That's exactly what this verse means; the readiness that comes from the gospel of peace. Being ready to endure with a peace that passes all understanding and a readiness to go and tell it on the mountain. These integuments are critical. See them in your mind as an internal garment, something that you wear all the time.

Verse 16 begins with *"In addition . . ."* to remind us that you can't use the defensive armor alone; you must use it in addition to the integuments we have just discussed. Paul says, in addition to everything I just told you, now I want you to pick up the shield of faith. This particular shield isn't the little round one that we often see in the movies. It's the Roman shield that was about four feet long by two-and-a-half-feet wide and about six inches thick.

That gives us a visual here that our faith must be long, wide, and solid so when the enemy is coming at us with the darts of temptation and the flaming arrows of destruction, we can say in faith, "No!" to lust, despair, discouragement and all the other weapons the enemy throws at us. That shield of faith protects us from getting wounded, because much like my surgery, it's often through an open wound that a parasite can crawl in. Our faith rises up and says, "Though I'm misunderstood, you see the real me;" "Though my teenager rages, even still I believe;" "Though there's no money in the bank, I will not despair."

With our hearts protected, now Paul turns our attention to our heads by telling us in verse 17 to take the helmet of salvation. *Take* the helmet means to receive it as a gift from the Lord; after all, our salvation is a gift, a free gift. It reminds us we have hope and it's in Jesus Christ alone. It also protects our minds from finding hope, meaning, and fulfillment in anything or anyone other than Jesus.

And right there, just that fast, we see the best defense is a good offense. Because before verse 17 comes to a close, we see Paul, under the anointing of the Holy Spirit, say when we receive the helmet from God himself, which gives us our hope, then we have the confidence to look the devil in the eye and begin speaking the Word of God. That, dear friend, is our sword, jabbed right into his Lake-of-Fire-doomed face.

The sword—our Bible, the Word of God—has all power especially, as it tells us in verse 18, when we pray in the Spirit. When the Word of God comes out of our mouths in the form of prayers, petitions, and requests, I believe that hell begins to shake. You see the enemy doesn't care if we go to church, but I believe that he takes notice when we start praying the Word of God.

Lastly, in verse 18, Paul ties it all together and puts a bow on it when he says, " . . . *with all this in mind, be alert and always keep on praying for all the saints.*" I believe he's saying, "Do everything I'm telling you to! Put on the full armor of God, but just in case your brother or sister in Christ forgets to put on their readiness shoes or take up their shield of faith, pray for them. Unify, come together, as not just one body, but one Church Body!"

What I find really interesting about all of this armor is that it's only to protect the front of the body. Aside from the helmet, there is absolutely nothing to cover the back. As I thought about it, I realized there is a very important reason for this. It's only in moving forward through the narrow gates of the Christian life that we are protected. But it's when we turn around and go our own way we become an open target for the enemy—because there is nothing on our backs to protect us. You see, Jesus is our rear guard, so we can be confident in going about the Lord's business—because *He* has our backs.

We must keep moving forward—no stopping—keeping our eyes and our ears open wide. Don't stop, don't turn around, and your armor will protect you against parasites in the Body of Christ.

# Epilogue

Just this evening, I was flipping through the channels on the TV when I came across a Discovery Channel show called *Monsters Inside Me*. It was a show about men and women who have had serious and sometimes deadly encounters with hosts of human-attacking parasites. At the conclusion of the show, biologist and host Dan Riskin said, "Parasites are found everywhere on the planet and the reason they've had success is because they are very effective at adapting to their environments. By hiding undetected inside their hosts, parasites are able to survive and reproduce. When a parasite dies, the host's immune system kicks in, often with devastating results. Let it be said that parasites are the ultimate suicide attackers."

It was frightening to see those little worms crawling inside a human being, creating rashes, severe pain, blindness, and death. It is even more frightening to see believers in Jesus Christ living so far below the abundant life they were saved to experience. Friends, the Lord wants you to be free of these deadly pests because free people help other people become free.

It is my prayer that you, through the power of true repentance, have become parasite-free. When the doctor told me the parasite in my body was dead, he said it had been cocooned within a tissue-like mass. The tissue wrapped the parasite with five distinct bands: four going in one direction and the fifth crossing over the other four. I couldn't help but think how much it reminded me of a human fist. It was as though Jesus himself, said "Oh, no. Not on my watch."

He'll do the same for you, if you'll just be willing to cry out to Him. You, my friend, are a tree of possibilities: *"A planting of the Lord for the display of His splendor"* (Isaiah 61:3).

It's time to get the worms out!